THE AWESOME POWER OF GOD

PRAYING ACCORDING TO THE PATTERN

By Sandy Sims & C.J. Thomas

Second Edition

Published by:
Sharing The Light Ministries
P.O. Box 596
Lithia Springs, GA 30122
www.myholycall.com

ISBN 0-9646515-1-3
Printed in the United States of America

All scripture quotations are taken from
The King James Version
(Bold, capitals, and italics added for emphasis)

Familiar definitions taken from "Strong's New Exhaustive
Concordance of the Bible" Copyright 1992. Word Bible
Publishers, Incorporated.

Illustrations from "The Tabernacle In the Wilderness"
Copyright © 1976, 1999 By Gerth Medien GmbH,
Asslar, Germany

Book cover design by Mark Hayes for
The Establishment Group
www.theestablishmentgroup.net

"Praying the Tabernacle Pattern is the removing of the veil which has separated the Church from the Holy of Holies for so long. I have personally had the privilege of ordaining, imparting to and speaking into the lives of Sandy and C.J. and can attest that their "Pattern" is straight from the throne! When the disciples asked Jesus to teach them to pray, this was that teaching."

Micheal Pipes
Next Move of God Ministries

Dedication

This book is dedicated to the
Father, Son and Holy Spirit.
Thank You for saving our lives and blessing us
to know Your heart and Your vision
for the Body of Christ and
the end-time harvest of souls.

We would also like to give special thanks to our loving
husbands, families, friends and intercessors.
We love you all and thank you
for your love and support.
Daily we pray God's richest
blessings upon you.

Preface

What we are about to share with you has been hidden in the Word and the heart of God for such a time as this!

This revelation is a gift from the Father to bless and unify the Body of Christ into His mighty invincible army. This corporate anointing will manifest the presence of God. Whether you are a part of the five-fold ministry, a seasoned Saint or a new convert in Christ, this revelation will bless God; bless you, and the world. It will also propel you into the Secret Place, the very presence of God!

We are God's end-time army, hand-picked, to bring in the final harvest and to fill the earth with His glory. In order to accomplish this task, WE MUST UNITE IN PRAYER! To the natural mind that seems impossible as we look at the landscape of all the different denominations and Church doctrines. However, with God—ALL THINGS ARE POSSIBLE!

Within this book you will see how the manifold wisdom of God has overcome denominational barriers. It has also overcome the gulf between Jew and Gentile, and every other obstacle to create His *"One New Man"* (Eph 2:15). The most spectacular element is the exponential multiplication (extremely rapid increase) of prayer power for the end-time harvest. Your royal priesthood enables you to pray for and on behalf of 6½ billion people! Yes, just one king-priest has that much power! Two king-priests produce 13 billion prayers. Three king-priests produce 19½ billion prayers. One can easily see **"The Awesome Power of God"** that will be released when the Church enters her king-priest ministry. Our God is a wise God!

To our Jewish brothers and sisters, true repentance by the Church and an apology has been long overdue. Therefore we stand in the gap and repent for all the atrocities that have happened to you throughout history by the Church. In addition, we repent for the actions of all others, past and present, inspired by satan to harm you.

We would also like to thank you for preserving the Word of God, keeping the Sabbaths, and celebrating the Feasts. The preservation of your rich heritage enabled us to see the manifold wisdom of God. You are truly God's chosen people and we thank you for being the vehicle through which God brought the Messiah to earth.

To our Gentile Christian brothers and sisters, we pray that you also have this heart of repentance and deep appreciation for the Jewish people. Whether or not they have received Jesus as Messiah, they need to know what an awesome blessing they have been. These heart attitudes create the foundation God needs to pour out His glory upon the entire earth! In John 17:21-22, Jesus prayed that we would be one so the world would know God sent His Son. He also said, if we became one the same glory upon Jesus would be upon us. This is the end-time glory everyone is waiting for—**THE AWESOME POWER OF GOD!**

Much Love, Blessings & Shalom!
Sandy Sims & C.J. Thomas

The Awesome Power Of God
Praying According To The Pattern

Contents

The Tabernacle Of Moses

The Tabernacle Foreshadows The Ministry Of Jesus

Ark of the Covenant

**Jesus the Carrier
of the Presence of God**

Altar of Incense

**Golden
Lampstand**

**Jesus the Apostle
and High Priest Who
makes our prayers
a sweet smelling
aroma unto God**

**Table of
Shewbread**

**Jesus the Light
of the World**

Brazen Laver

**Jesus the Bread
of the Life**

**Jesus the Word
of God made flesh**

Brazen Altar

**Jesus the sinless Lamb
became the Eternal Sacrifice**

The High Priest Of Israel

Foreword

This book provides revelation on the most important aspect of Christianity, which is prayer. The teaching by Jesus in Matthew 6:9-13, the Lord's Prayer, is a model or pattern for prayer. Revelation 1:5-6 states that by the Blood of Jesus we have been made *"kings and priests"* unto God. According to I Peter 2:9, we are a *"royal priesthood"* to show forth the praises of our God. Within the Tabernacle of Moses there are shadow pictures that show a relationship between the model prayer and our royal priesthood.

Understanding the true meaning and the correlation between the Lord's model prayer, the Tabernacle and our royal priesthood will bring in the glory of God and His end-time harvest of souls!

The Tabernacle of Moses is one of the most spectacular creations that God has given to mankind. Just to give you a brief description of how important it is, let's examine the scriptures. Exodus 25:8 states that God told Moses to build Him a Tabernacle so that He could come and dwell with them. The Tabernacle of God made it possible for the holiness of God to dwell with man upon the earth. Hebrews 8:2 tells us that the Tabernacle of Moses is a replica of the true Tabernacle in heaven and that Jesus is the High Priest and Minister of that Tabernacle. The Tabernacle of Moses is a shadow picture of the life, death, resurrection, and total dominion of Jesus Christ. Every detail of the Tabernacle testifies of Jesus Christ, the Lamb of God!

Jesus is our great King and High Priest ministering in the heavenly Tabernacle. And He has made us king-priests; therefore we should learn how to fulfill this ministry. The truths in this book show that the Tabernacle of Moses is an awesome Prayer Pattern. And this Tabernacle Prayer will enable us to fulfill our holy calling to be king-priests unto God, our glorious destiny!

Chapter One

Introduction

God, through Moses His prophet, commanded Pharaoh to let His people go so they may worship Him. Through God's mighty hand, the Israelites were delivered from slavery in Egypt. In the wilderness of Sinai, Moses was given precise instructions by God to build a Tabernacle, a place to worship and serve Him. In Exodus 25:8 the Lord said, *"And let them make me a sanctuary; that I may dwell among them"*.

The building of the Tabernacle was for the purpose of God dwelling among His people. He gave His people a way to receive atonement for their sins, and a method of approach to Him. In God's manifold wisdom He also made everything within the Tabernacle a shadow picture prophesying the life and ministry of the Lord Jesus Christ—the Lamb of God. Glory to God, the Tabernacle not only stands as a testimony of God's plan of redemption, but also gives us the perfect way to worship Him!

Let's begin our study of the Prayer Pattern with the linen gate that surrounded the Tabernacle of Moses. This is where we repent and enter God's gates with thanksgiving and His courts with praise. The first piece of furniture within the Tabernacle was the Brazen Altar where the animals were sacrificed. This is symbolic of Jesus, the Lamb of God, Who took away the sins of the world on the Brazen Altar of Calvary. We praise Jesus for shedding His Blood and redeeming us.

The second piece of furniture was the Brazen Laver. It was a basin of water where the priests would wash before ministering unto the Lord. At this Laver we thank Him that He is the Word made flesh and that we are washed by the water of His Word.

The next piece of furniture was the Candlestick or Lampstand. It is symbolic of Jesus, the Light of the world, anointed with the power of the Holy Spirit. At the Candlestick we thank Jesus that He gave us the gift of the Holy Spirit so we would be a reflection of His great light.

The following piece of furniture was the Table of Shewbread, with four corners, surrounded by a golden crown. It housed the twelve loaves of Shewbread, which were symbolic of the Jewish nation. The Table now represents the four corners of the earth and the Shewbread represents all the people upon God's heart. It is here we enter into our role as intercessors, standing in the gap and repenting for all men.

Next we have the Altar of Incense, which represents the fragrance of *"true worship"*. We thank Jesus for perfecting our prayers and making them a sweet smelling perfume unto the Father. This allows us to go beyond the veil and enter into the presence of God.

At the Ark of the Covenant (Mercy Seat), we worship Father, Son and Holy Spirit and experience perfect communion. This is not only the perfect way to pray and worship the Lord but it will manifest **"The Awesome Power of God!"**

I Peter 2:9
But ye are a chosen generation, a royal priesthood, an holy nation, a peculiar people; that ye should shew forth the praises of him who hath called you out of darkness into his marvellous light:

For years we have read, quoted, and sang these words without understanding their importance. First Peter 2:9 is a powerful scripture that holds the key to ushering in the glory of God and the completion of all things He has purposed for mankind. Yes, the key to manifesting the glory is in this scripture, yet even more startling is the fact that the key to this scripture is you! YOU are the key, not the Church as a whole, not your pastor, your prayer group, your mother, father, husband, wife, sister, brother or neighbor—but Y-O-U!

In the Old Testament the high priest would go into the presence of God once a year to make atonement for Israel. Just as it was the duty of the high priest in the Old Testament to enter into the presence of God alone, yet on behalf of all, YOU have also been entrusted with that same power and responsibility. Revelation 1:5-6 says that the *"Prince of the kings of the earth"* has made us kings and priests unto God. This calling is not optional, if you are a child of God washed by the Blood of Jesus, you have been made a king and a priest. Whether you are a part of the five-fold ministry or a new convert, the first call of God upon your life is to be a king and priest unto Him!

The alarming aspect of this call is that most of us have never been taught the functions or duties of these offices! By the prompting of the Holy Spirit, we began to search the scriptures and receive revelation from Him concerning the requirements of this holy calling. As kings, we are to declare and decree the Word of God, live as royalty and reign with dominion, authority and power. As priests, we are to live holy and become the intercessors God desires to stand in the gap for all men. Furthermore, we are to have communion and fellowship with the Lord and worship Him in spirit and in truth.

Praying according to the divine order of the Tabernacle of Moses will bless you with each accomplishment. This book will plant your feet firmly on the right path to become what all creation has been waiting for—THE MANIFESTED SONS OF GOD! It will also open up to you a treasure house of knowledge and information that will inspire you to fulfill your destiny.

The main reason why we have not fulfilled this holy calling is because we have not understood our adoption. We have been adopted into Jesus' family. Jesus was born Jewish, in Israel, and we have been adopted into the Lord's family. Yet unfortunately we know little or nothing about this beautiful heritage we have been given. We act as if Jesus had been adopted into our family instead of us being adopted into His! In the United States, we have *"Americanized"* Jesus! We have taken Him out of Israel, divorced Him from His people and we know nothing about His customs or ways.

Another important point is that primarily Jewish people wrote the Bible. Without knowing their culture or having a true interpretation of their language, it is impossible to know what the Bible is truly saying. In order to rightly divide the Word of God and fully understand our Lord Jesus Christ, we must have a basic understanding of Jewish culture, customs and their language.

Let's look at the adoption issue from a different angle. If you adopted a child would you let that child come into your house, take over and tell you how to worship? Absolutely not! Children don't have the wisdom or knowledge to run their own lives let alone yours. Usually an adopted child would respect you and learn to obey the rules of your household and become an integral part of your family. We have never done this—the Church has been a rebellious child so to speak! We have entered Jesus' household but have never taken the time to learn about our Jewish heritage, love our Jewish brethren and pray for them.

This Jewish family we have been adopted into has a way of worship that will manifest the presence of God. God Himself, thousands of years ago, established this way of worship. However, we have not entered into that way of worship or taken the time to learn about it. In this book you will learn how to pray and worship God according to His divine will.

The Tabernacle of Moses is also a prophetic timeline for the history of the Church. Each piece of the Tabernacle represents spiritual times and seasons. When the Reformation (1500's) restored the truth that we are saved by faith in Christ alone, the Brazen Altar was reinstated. The Wesley Brothers (1700's) taught the truth of sanctification by the Word, which represents the Laver. The Azusa Street revival in the early 1900's gave us a greater revelation of the Person of Jesus Christ and His anointing, which is represented by the

Candlestick. The Charismatic movement in the 1960's, with emphasis on the Holy Spirit and His gifts, restored the Table of Shewbread. We are now in the process of restoring the Altar of Incense, where we become true worshippers unto the Lord and respond to Him as *"Daddy"* our loving Father. True worship allows us to be transported into the Holy of Holies the very presence of God.

This phase is called the *"Saints Movement"*. In this movement Christians become true worshippers, who worship the Lord in spirit and in truth, and manifest His glory in the earth. Get ready for a complete transformation! As you become one of the greatly sought after worshippers, your life will blossom with the awesome power and presence of God!

In praying according to Pattern, you will notice tremendous growth in all areas of your life. There is also awesome power generated in a corporate setting as Saints unify as one, under the Word of God. The most exciting benefit is that you will be a vital part of God fulfilling His end-time plans and purposes. We are on the threshold of the most exciting time in human history! Don't you know that you were born to the kingdom for such a time as this! You will not want to miss your part in bringing forth the awesome power of God's glory in these last days. The Word promises that the knowledge of His glory will cover the earth as the waters cover the sea, causing the most awesome revival this world has ever seen! This revival will glorify our Father in the earth; bring about the salvation of multitudes of lost souls and the perfection of the Saints! We know that your joy will be full, when you see the rewards of your choice in eternity!

WARNING TO THE CASUAL READER!

If you don't want to be a vital part of God's army in preparation for the glory of God and the Second Coming of Christ...

LAY THIS BOOK DOWN IMMEDIATELY, DO NOT CONTINUE PAST THIS PAGE!!

However, for the rest of you who are as hungry and eager to please the Lord as we are, let's quickly begin our journey into the knowledge of His will. Take a good look at yourself now, because you will not be the same person by the time you finish this book.

Sandy & C.J.

Chapter Two

The Tabernacle
God's Divine Order

The Tabernacle

Ps 16:11
Thou wilt show me the path of life: in thy presence is fulness of joy; at thy right hand there are pleasures for evermore.

The Tabernacle Prayer is fashioned in the Pattern of the Tabernacle of Moses (Hebrews 9:1-5). The Tabernacle of Moses consisted of the Outer Court, entered at the east, with the Brazen Altar of Sacrifice and the Brazen Laver. The Inner Court, where only the priests could go, consisted of the Golden Candlestick (south), Table of Shewbread (north), and the Altar of Incense (west). The Altar of Incense stood directly in front of the veil that separated the Inner Court from the Most Holy Place. The Most Holy Place was where the manifest presence of God (Glory Cloud) dwelt. It dwelt between the Cherubim above the Mercy Seat, the cover to the Ark of the Covenant. Only the High Priest had access to the Most Holy Place or Holy of Holies once a year, on the Day of Atonement. At that special time he offered the blood of the sacrifice for the sins of Israel.

The divine order of worship that God gave to Moses made it possible for Him to dwell among His people. In other words, God showed Moses how to receive and retain His presence. God is the same yesterday, today, and forever. Therefore, the revelation that He gave to Moses is equally important to us as New Testament believers. When Jesus died and the veil of the Most Holy Place was rent from top to bottom, He was showing us that He had provided access for us to enter His presence. This act was in fact a beacon light to guide us to the most important accomplishment in life – to enter into the very presence of God!

When God described creation He did it in three chapters, but when God described the Tabernacle He did it in such great detail that it took over one hundred chapters! Knowledge of the Tabernacle is extremely important because the Tabernacle is not only a replica of the true Tabernacle in heaven (Hebrews 8:1-2), but it is the type and shadow of Jesus Christ. Throughout the book of Revelation, which reveals our final destiny, we are shown that there is a Temple in heaven. We were created for the "timeless" ministry of worshipping our Lord in this place.

The Tabernacle was constructed for the atonement of sins and the reverence, honor and worship of God. In the Old Testament the people brought animals to be sacrificed. Today, as New Testament believers, we are to bring the sacrifice of praise. Praise is important because where there is praise and worship of the Lord; there He will be in the midst. Psalms 22:3 states that God inhabits our praises. The word *"inhabit";* means to sit down, dwell, and to marry. When we praise the Lord, He sits down, and dwells with us and we experience an intimate relationship with our Creator. When it comes to praise most people think that praise is singing songs or declaring, *"I praise You Lord"*, and *"I praise You Jesus"*. In order to praise Him properly, we must know what He has accomplished. If we don't know what He has done, how can we truly praise Him? True praise is not cheap; it will cost us something. We will have to study the Word of God to know what He has done, and then declare it.

Many people don't want to pay the price to learn or write down scriptures. How is it that we can do whatever it takes to learn new things for our jobs, hobbies, or worldly things, but when it comes to the things of God we are very quick to say; "it doesn't take all of that"? How would you feel if someone's job involved announcing you and all of your lifetime achievements, but that person never took the time to learn about you? Needless to say, when they got up to announce your achievements it was shallow, incomplete and didn't even begin to show the world what you had done. That is the way many of us would introduce God! Jesus has given us the job to *"shew"* forth His praises yet most of us don't know or cannot recite what He has done for us.

The Tabernacle, also called the *"Tabernacle of Testimony"*, testifies of the Lord Jesus Christ. The Word tells us in Revelation 12:11, that we overcome the devil by the Blood of the Lamb, and by the word of our testimony. We have interpreted that scripture to mean our own personal testimony. Our personal testimonies are a tremendous blessing to others, but it will not stop the hordes of hell from destroying us. The word *"testimony"* comes from a root word that means, *"martyr"*. That scripture is saying we overcome the devil by the Blood of the Lamb and by our testimony of the life, death, resurrection and total dominion of Jesus Christ! Therefore, as we testify of Jesus from the front gate all the way into the Holy of Holies, we are destroying the enemy. According to Psalms 8:2, God has ordained praise to silence the enemy and the avenger.

The Tabernacle also shows us the divine order of worship that produces power. When the priests performed their ministry in the Tabernacle, they did it according to the explicit instruction given by Moses. They could not haphazardly minister in the Tabernacle. If this order were not strictly followed, instant death would occur. The order was necessary for the protection of the life of the priest. Today, because of God's mercy and the Blood of Jesus, we don't die physically. However, there is a type of spiritual death that occurs when we don't follow divine order. This spiritual death makes our prayers become less effective or null and void. This same principle happened to the Israelites in the days of Isaiah. The Prophet Isaiah, in Chapter 58, was instructed to tell the Israelites that their fasting and prayers were futile because they had ignored the ordinance of God.

Isa 58:1-2
Cry aloud, spare not, lift up thy voice like a trumpet, and shew my people their transgression, and the house of Jacob their sins. Yet they seek me daily, and delight to know my ways, as a nation that did righteousness, and FORSOOK NOT THE ORDINANCE OF THEIR GOD: they ask of me the ordinances of justice; they take delight in approaching to God.

In verse 6 of this same chapter God tells them what He expects from prayer and fasting if done according to His will.

Isa 58:6
Is not this the fast that I have chosen? To loose the bands of wickedness, to undo heavy burdens, and to let the oppressed go free, and that ye break every yoke?

Because they forsook the ordinance, which means the ceremony, fashion, and due order in their approach to God, they were powerless! In retrospect, if we pray according to the due order, fashion and ceremony He has set, we will have the power to loose the bands of wickedness, undo heavy burdens, let the oppressed go free, and break every yoke!

God told Moses seven times to make the Tabernacle according to pattern! The number seven denotes perfection or fullness. When we pray in perfect harmony with the divine order of God, we will produce the fullness of His glory! Concluding Chapter 58, God indicates that if we are **NOT GOING OUR OWN WAY OR SPEAKING OUR OWN WORDS**, then we will delight ourselves in Him and ride upon the High Places (Isaiah 58:14). In praying according to Pattern, you cannot go your own way or speak your own words because you pray the Word of God! God's divine order of prayer removes selfishness, delivers us from telling God what we think He ought to do, and most importantly we accomplish our objective because His Word will not return void!

Pray After This Manner

In Matthew 6:9-13, Jesus was giving instructions on how to pray. He said; **"AFTER THIS MANNER THEREFORE PRAY."** Jesus was giving us a model or pattern for prayer. This means that we should follow the points brought out in the pattern. Prayer, *"AFTER THIS MANNER"*, is in the exact Pattern of the Tabernacle of Moses! **"Our Father which art in heaven, Hallowed be thy name"**, represents repentance and entering His gates with thanksgiving and His courts with praise. **"Thy kingdom come"**, represents the Altar of Sacrifice. Jesus, through His life, death and resurrection, brought the Kingdom of God to the earth. **"Thy will be done"**, represents the Laver (the Word) because God's will is His Word. The statement **"in earth, as it is in heaven"**, represents the Golden Candlestick which is the anointing and power of the Holy Spirit. The Holy Spirit will cause God's will to be done on earth as it is in heaven. **"Give us this day our daily bread, And forgive our debts as we forgive our debtors"**, represents the Table of Shewbread. This is where we repent for the world, spiritually receive communion, and intercede. We, as king-priests, must stand in the gap and repent for all men so God can bring blessing and not judgment. **"And lead us not into temptation, but deliver us from evil"** represents the Altar of Incense where we purge our hearts and worship the Lord in spirit and in truth. **"For thine is the kingdom, and the power, and the glory, for ever, A-men"**, represents the Most Holy Place where we see the manifest Glory of God and worship Him. Hallelujah! As you can see there is a divine order of prayer that God desires. The Pattern of the Tabernacle of Moses and the instruction by Jesus to pray *"after this manner"*, are in perfect harmony and clearly show divine order!

Jesus Is The Tabernacle

John 14:1-6
Let not your heart be troubled: ye believe in God, believe also in me. In my Father's house there are many mansions: if it were not so, I would have told you. I go to prepare a place for you. And if I go and prepare a place for you, I will come again, and receive you unto myself; that where I am, there ye may be also. And wither I go ye know, and the way ye know. THOMAS SAITH UNTO HIM, LORD, WE KNOW NOT WITHER THOU GOEST; AND HOW CAN WE KNOW THE WAY? JESUS SAITH UNTO HIM, I AM THE WAY, THE TRUTH, AND THE LIFE: NO MAN COMETH UNTO THE FATHER, BUT BY ME.

Jesus was telling his disciples that He was going to His Father's house and would prepare a place (dwelling place) for them. It is interesting to note that Jesus also told them that they knew where He was going and the way to get there! The answer of Jesus in verse 6 was in direct response to the question of Thomas; "we do not know where You are going, and how can we know the way?" In John 14:6, Jesus said, I AM THE WAY, THE TRUTH AND THE LIFE AND NO MAN COMES TO THE FATHER BUT BY ME. The Jews understood that He was speaking of the pathway through the Tabernacle. The entrances to the Outer and Inner courts and the Holy of Holies were known as the WAY, the TRUTH, and the LIFE. Jesus was saying I AM THE TABERNACLE!

He was also confirming that there is a divine order of prayer that must be followed in order to get into the presence of the Father. In these scriptures, we have always thought that Jesus was just talking about taking us to heaven someday, and they can certainly be interpreted that way. However, Jesus was also saying that He has prepared a *"dwelling place"* for each of us where we can enter and abide in His presence, THROUGH

PRAYER! When we enter His gates with thanksgiving and His Courts with praise, and continue to praise and worship our way into the Holy of Holies, we find ourselves abiding in God's presence!

Chapter Three

The Power Of
The Word Of God

One of the main reasons that God has called all men to a king-priest ministry is the fact that nothing is established on this earth unless it is spoken first.

John 1:1-3
In the beginning was the Word, and the Word was with God, and the Word was God. The same was in the beginning with God. All things were made by him; and without him was not any thing made that was made.

Absolutely nothing in heaven or earth was made without the Word of God. We can clearly see this truth in Genesis Chapter one as God spoke the Word and all things were created. We, being made in His likeness and image, also must speak the Word of God so it can be established in our lives and upon this earth. That is why we are told in I Peter 2:9, that we should *"shew"* forth the praises of God Who has delivered us from darkness, and has brought us into His light. The word *"shew"* means to publish and celebrate the origin and completion of the promises of God. When we do this we will be establishing His promises in our lives and upon this earth.

When we read about the glory, anointing, and the power of God, most Christians automatically assume that the Bible is only talking to the five-fold ministry. Many Christians never expect to walk in this anointing even though Jesus told us that we would do greater works than He did. This deception is one of the main power tools of the devil. As long as he can keep us ignorant of the plan and purposes of God for our lives, he can continue to kill, steal and destroy. We are to be what all creation groans for—the manifested sons of God who will destroy the works of the devil. We are ALL to walk in the glory and power of God! God is coming back for a glorious Church not just a glorious few. But without the revelation and declaration of God's Word, we will not walk in that power! This next scripture gives us a greater understanding of why it's important for us to enter into our king-priest ministry to claim the anointing and the promises of God.

Beholding The Glory

II Cor 3:18
But we all, with OPEN FACE beholding as in a glass the glory of the Lord, are changed into the same image from glory to glory, even as by the Spirit of the Lord.

Before addressing the body of this scripture, we will explain the words *"open face"* which means to have revelation knowledge and understanding. Preceding this verse Paul tells us that a veil blinded the minds of the people when they read the Old Testament. He also said that even when Moses is read today, there is a veil over their hearts. The word *"veil"* means to cover-up, conceal or keep secret. Paul was saying there are many things that are hidden and kept secret in the reading of the Old Testament and of Moses. Ask God right now to remove the veil from your heart and mind so you can understand the powerful truths He has hidden within the Tabernacle of Moses. Jesus expressed just how important the writings of Moses are in this next scripture.

John 5:46-47
For had ye believed Moses, ye would have believed me: for he wrote of me. But if ye believe not his writings, how shall ye believe my words?

Jesus is saying if you don't believe what Moses wrote about me, how can you believe what I say? How did Moses write about Jesus? Moses wrote the first five books of the Bible, part of which he details the building of the Tabernacle! The Tabernacle tells of the accomplishments, attributes, characteristics and the glory of God in Jesus Christ. Understanding and declaring that Jesus is the fulfillment of the Tabernacle, will manifest His glory. When we pray according to Pattern we declare Who He is and who we are in Him.

In other words, when we with *"open face"* (understanding), behold the glory of the Lord as in a mirror, we are changed into that same image! We must see ourselves with the glory! That is how it is manifested. This is the same principle that God used with Abram and Sarai to bring forth His promises. During the day, the dust of the ground reminded them of the promise that God would greatly multiply their descendants. And at night the number of stars also reminded them. As if that wasn't enough, God renamed Abram to Abraham and Sarai to Sarah so that they would hear and speak the promise that they were to be the father and mother of many nations.

In order to receive the promises of God, we must constantly see, hear and speak of their completion in our lives. Praying according to Pattern simultaneously accomplishes all these things. There are so many benefits to praying in this manner that it would take volumes to list. Another important reason why we should pray according to Pattern is because we are forced to pray the Word of God. When we pray the Word of God change is inevitable because within the Word is the power to sanctify, cleanse and manifest His glory.

The Cleansing Power Of The Word

Eph 5:26-27
That he might SANCTIFY and CLEANSE it with the WASHING of WATER by the WORD, That he might present it to himself a glorious church, not having spot, or wrinkle, or any such thing; but that it should be holy and without blemish.

The word *"sanctify"*, means to make holy, purify or consecrate. It also means to make physically pure or morally blameless. The word *"cleanse"* means to make clean, purge and purify. The Word of God will not only clean, but it will purge you by getting rid of the junk that lies deep within. The word *"washing"* means a bath. It also means to cleanse the face, hands, feet and garments. The Word of God will bathe you so that you can face all things without guilt. It will bathe your hands and feet so that your works and your walk will be clean. It will also wash your garments so you can become a priest unto God and intercede for others. The word *"water"* means to rain as in a shower. The Word of God is a rain shower – a shower of power! The Word of God has the power to cleanse, purify and sanctify. The only way to be transformed into the glorious Church is **BY THE WASHING OF WATER BY THE WORD**!

Praying According To Pattern Builds Faith

The Word tells us that without faith it is impossible to please God (Hebrews 11:6). Romans 10:17 tells us that faith comes by hearing and hearing by the Word of God. This double reference to hearing tells us that we must continue to hear the Word of God in order to build faith. It also tells us that faith, the assurance and belief in the Word, comes by two different types of *"hearing"*. As defined in the Greek, the first is **receptive**; the act of hearing, being part of the audience. The second type is **active;** to give or to report.

With this Prayer Pattern, you will be performing both kinds of hearing at the same time. You will be speaking the Word and hearing the Word simultaneously, thereby building faith! As you do this daily, you will experience a new level of faith and intimacy with God that you never knew was possible. You will come to understand the scriptures more clearly as God pours out revelation upon you concerning His Word. You will also experience a greater anointing, a deeper fellowship, and true communion with the Father. Never again will you experience a dry, unproductive prayer time. You will be in the presence of the Lord – the Secret Place of the Most High!

Chapter Four

The Manifested Glory Of God

God has declared that His glory shall cover the earth as the waters cover the sea. Just imagine the glory of God saturating the earth like that! The presence of God in current revivals can be classified as *"visitation"* not *"habitation"*. True habitation would bring to pass the words that Jesus spoke over us in John 14:12, *"The works that I do shall he do also; and greater works than these shall he do"*. In addition miracles, signs and wonders would break out everywhere, not just in the Church but also in our homes, schools, workplaces, and on our streets.

Let's look at the Word concerning how David brought the Ark or the presence of God into Jerusalem. The first time David tried to bring the Ark of the Covenant into the city it ended in disaster with the death of Uzzah (I Chronicles 13:10).

I Chron 13:13-14
So David brought not the ark home to himself to the city of David, but carried it aside into the house of Obededom the Gittite. And the ark of God remained with the family of Obededom in his house three months. And the LORD blessed the house of Obededom, and all that he had.

The Ark of the Covenant was at Obededom's house blessing only him and his household. David was determined to bring the Ark into Jerusalem so it could bless the entire nation. Prophetically this is the state of the Church today. The Ark of God's presence is in a *"house"* blessing a few people, which are the revivals. However, we need the Ark to come to the entire Church, spiritual Jerusalem, so it can bless the world! Well let's discover how David succeeded in bringing the Ark into Jerusalem.

I Chron 15:1
And David made him houses in the city of David, and prepared a place for the ark of God, and pitched for it a tent.

On David's first attempt we did not see where he prepared a tent for the Ark, a place where God could dwell. There **MUST BE A PLACE** for the presence of God to dwell! We serve a holy God and He can't dwell just anywhere. In Exodus 25:8 the Lord said, *"And let them make me a sanctuary; that I may dwell among them"*. If we want God to come and dwell among us we must build him a sanctuary or tabernacle. Ephesians 2:22, states that we are to build God a habitation in our spirits.

Another critical aspect that David overlooked the first time is found in the following scriptures.

I Chron 15:2
Then David said, NONE OUGHT TO CARRY THE ARK OF GOD BUT THE LEVITES: for them hath the LORD chosen to carry the ark of God, and to minister unto him for ever.

I Chron 15:12-15
And said unto them, Ye are the chief of the fathers of the Levites: sanctify yourselves, both ye and your brethren, that ye may bring up the ark of the LORD God of Israel unto the place that I have prepared for it. For because ye did it not at the first, the LORD our God made a breach upon us, for that we sought him not after the DUE ORDER. So the priests and the Levites sanctified themselves to bring up the ark of the LORD God of Israel. And the children of the Levites bare the ark of God upon their shoulders with the staves thereon, as Moses commanded according to the word of the LORD.

The presence of God can only be brought in on the shoulders of the priests. Please note that because they did not follow the *"due order"* it not only brought death, but the Ark could not be brought into Jerusalem. Another account of David's second effort to bring the Ark to Jerusalem in II Samuel further proves this fact.

II Sam 6:13-14
And it was so, that when they that bare the ark of the LORD had gone six paces, he sacrificed oxen and fatlings. And David danced before the LORD with all his might; and David was girded with a linen ephod.

Every six steps they sacrificed an animal and worshipped the Lord. The number six represents man. Prophetically this scripture is saying that there are divine steps of worship that a man can take that will bring the presence of God into spiritual Jerusalem! Furthermore David, a king, wearing a linen ephod clearly showed us that it will take a <u>KING AND A PRIEST</u> to bring in the presence of the Lord! The glory of God everyone is looking for and all creation is groaning for, can only be brought in on the shoulders of the KING-PRIESTS!!! We must enter into our king-priest ministry if we expect to see the glory come to the Church!

Just imagine how long it took to bring the Ark into Jerusalem. Also imagine the repentance, blood, fire and worship that marked the trail from Obededom's house to the City of David. We, the Church, must quickly enter our king-priest ministry and pray according to Pattern until one day we reach our destination of "heavenly Jerusalem"-- manifesting the presence of God!

The Former And Latter Rain

The main reason that God desires for us to pray according to Pattern is because of the awesome power within this Prayer Pattern to bring in the end-time harvest of souls. Every harvest physical or spiritual must be accomplished by the collective power of God and man, and must also receive the two vital elements of sun and rain. In the natural man cultivates the ground, plants the seed, protects the crops, and then reaps the harvest when full grown. God supplies the sun and rain necessary for the harvest.

Likewise in the spirit realm man cultivates the ground, which is his heart by repentance. He then plants the Word of God within it, protects the Word, and then harvests that Word when it is fully-grown. According to James 5:7, *"the husbandman waiteth for the precious fruit of the earth, and hath long patience for it, until he receive the early and latter rain"*. Job 36:27 tells us that rain is poured down on the earth according to the vapor thereof. Water originates on the earth and when heated it evaporates and becomes vapor. The vapors rise and form a cloud. The cloud gets close to the sun and the light from the sun (lightning) strikes the cloud and rain falls upon the earth. Rain is dependent upon the vapor sent up. IF THERE IS NO VAPOR—THERE WILL BE NO RAIN!

Jesus told the woman at the well that if she knew the gift of God and Who was standing before her, she would ask and He would give her living water. He also said in John 7:38, that all that believe on Him, out of their innermost being shall flow rivers of living water. The word *"water"* in the Greek means to rain, especially a shower. The water that Jesus gave us is FOR THE PRODUCTION OF RAIN! When heat is applied by the worship of God, by His Word and according to Pattern, evaporation takes place and vapors are released. Evaporation will not take place if we are lukewarm, nor can evaporation take place with our own words. It can only take place by the S-O-N, the Word of God!

As we worship the Lord by His Word, the vapors of true worship rise and form a cloud. As the cloud moves closer to the S-O-N, He reaches out and strikes the cloud and blessings rain down upon the earth. TRUE WORSHIP BRINGS THE RAIN. Now let's revisit James 5:7 where it states that the *"Husbandman"* is waiting until He receives the former and latter rain. Jesus is waiting for us to send up the vapors of true worship according to the Old Testament divine order of worship as New Testament kings and priests. THE FORMER AND LATTER RAIN IS DEPENDENT UPON US! We have been waiting for God to send the former and latter rain and He has been waiting for us to send up the vapors! NO VAPOR—NO RAIN!

Joel 2:23
Be glad then, ye children of Zion, and rejoice in the Lord your God: for he hath given you the former rain moderately, and he will cause to come down for you the rain, the former rain, and the latter rain in the first month.

There are two main rainy seasons in Israel, the autumn and spring rains, separated by several months of dry weather. The autumn rain is the former rain and the spring rain is the latter rain. Since the early 1990's, the two rainy seasons have collided so now there is continual rain in Israel. The former rain was a selective rain while the latter rain covered a widespread area. The Church, spiritual Israel, prophetically parallels whatever happens in physical Israel. Right now in the Body of Christ, we have selective rain or revival, but God has promised widespread rain and a supernatural harvest after the former and latter rain fall *"together"* in the first month (Joel 2:23).

New Testament king-priests sending up true worship vapors according to the Old Testament divine order will bring about the collision of the two rains! The result will be worldwide revival!

Joel 2:23-25, tells us that when the former and latter rains fall together, the harvest will be plentiful even restoring the years that the locust, cankerworm, caterpillar, and palmerworm has eaten. His Spirit shall come upon all flesh, and whoever shall call upon the name of the Lord shall be delivered (Joel 2:32). Yes, the harvest depends upon us! When we realize the importance of our king-priest ministry and send up the vapors of true worship, God will send the former and latter rain!

Jerusalem, The Place Of Worship

John 4:20-22
Our fathers worshipped in this mountain; and ye say, that in Jerusalem is the place where men ought to worship. Jesus saith unto her, Woman, believe me, the hour cometh, when ye shall neither in this mountain, nor yet at Jerusalem, worship the Father. YE WORSHIP YE KNOW NOT WHAT: WE KNOW WHAT WE WORSHIP: FOR SALVATION IS OF THE JEWS.

The woman at the well makes a statement concerning the place of worship. She says that her fathers worshipped in Samaria, but the Jews say that they should worship in Jerusalem. In John 4:21, Jesus responds by telling her there would come a day when she would not worship God in Samaria or Jerusalem. But He makes a very interesting point in verse 22. Jesus tells her, in effect, that "YOU DON'T KNOW WHAT YOU ARE DOING, YOU DON'T KNOW WHAT YOU ARE WORSHIPPING! WE JEWS, KNOW WHAT WE ARE WORSHIPPING BECAUSE SALVATION IS OF THE JEWS." HE WAS CONFIRMING THE JEWISH WAY OF WORSHIP – and this divine order of worship brings salvation or deliverance!

What did Jesus mean when He told her that she was worshipping what she did not know? If we examine the history of this woman's ancestors and their worship in Samaria, we find that her fathers were in rebellion against God. The Lord had a united kingdom of Israel under King David. His son Solomon became king at his death. After King Solomon's death, the kingdom of Israel was separated into the Northern and Southern kingdoms. Rehoboam, Solomon's son was king of the Southern kingdom (two tribes). Jeroboam was made king of the Northern kingdom (ten tribes) and he set up worship in the cities and hills of Samaria (I Kings 12).

According to Leviticus 23, the Jewish males were required to appear in Jerusalem three times a year to celebrate God's Feasts. They were Passover, Pentecost, and Tabernacles. Jeroboam made two golden calves and set them up in Bethel and Dan, leading the Northern tribes into idolatry (I Kings 12:29). He told them it was too much for them to go up to Jerusalem to worship, so he established a counterfeit Feast of Tabernacles. The first Feast, Passover, was a celebration of deliverance from Egypt, or the old life of bondage. Pentecost, the second Feast held fifty days later, marked the date that God gave the ten commandments (law) in the wilderness of Sinai. The Feast of Tabernacles was the third and final Feast of the year to thank God for supernatural provision in the wilderness and to celebrate the final ingathering of the harvest.

These Feasts also symbolize our spiritual walk with God and they are in the exact pattern of the Tabernacle. Passover is our salvation by the Blood of Jesus Christ (Outer Court). Pentecost is our baptism in the Holy Spirit, where He writes His laws upon our hearts (Inner Court). The Feast of Tabernacles signifies our entrance into the fullness of our king-priest ministry (Holy of Holies). And as king-priests, we worship in "spirit and in truth" and bring the rain needed for the final harvest.

The scripture states that Jeroboam imitated the Feast of Tabernacles only. Not understanding the significance, I asked the Lord why Jeroboam only imitated the Feast of Tabernacles and not the other two. His answer astounded me, He said; *"The enemy doesn't care if you get saved and filled with the Holy*

Spirit, because even then he is able to make many Christians ineffective. But what the enemy hates and desperately does not want, is for you to go past the Inner Court and become king-priests that go up to Heavenly Jerusalem to worship Me! Because when this happens YOU WILL BRING THE FORMER AND LATTER RAIN and the enemy's fate will be sealed!"

Idolatrous worship was set up in Samaria in direct rebellion to worshipping God in the manner and divine order that He had set forth. Jeroboam told the Northern Tribes that it was too much for them to follow God's ordinance and go up to Jerusalem. So when you hear that voice saying *"it's too much for you to pray according to Pattern or it doesn't take all of that"*, you will certainly know the enemy's motivation! Is it any wonder that Jesus told this woman at the well that she did not know what she was worshipping?

In John 4:21, He tells her there would come a time when she would not worship in Samaria or Jerusalem. In verse 23, He further states that the true worshippers would worship God in spirit and in truth. In order for us to worship God in spirit and in truth, we must understand what that really means. Let's examine what it means to worship in spirit. Jesus Christ saved us with His Blood and gave us the Holy Spirit. Worshipping God in spirit is to worship in our spirits by the grace of the Holy Spirit. Worshipping in truth is to worship Him with the Word of God (truth) according to His will. Therefore, worshipping in spirit and in truth is worshipping God in our spirit, with the truth of His Word, in divine order!

In John 4:22 Jesus said, in effect, THE JEWS HAVE THE DIVINE ORDER OF WORSHIP AND I AM THE FULFILLMENT, THE WORD OF GOD! The divine order of worship did not change only the place of worship! Because of the cross of Calvary and the gift of the Holy Spirit, we don't have to go to physical Jerusalem to worship the Lord. We can now worship God in the spirit realm in heavenly Jerusalem. Praying the Tabernacle Prayer, declaring Jesus as the fulfillment of every part of the Tabernacle, gives us the power to become true worshippers unto God!

The Father Is Seeking You!

John 4:23-24
But the hour cometh, and now is, when the true worshippers shall worship the Father in spirit and in truth: for the Father seeketh such to worship him. God is a Spirit: and they that worship him must worship him in spirit and in truth.

In John 4:23, Jesus says that the Father is seeking true worshippers who will worship Him in spirit and in truth. Are you one of the precious worshippers God is searching for to bring in the end-time harvest of souls, the precious fruit of the earth? Are you going to fulfill your calling to be a king-priest unto God, or will you let tradition and unbelief rob you of great eternal rewards? The choice is yours my friend. Yet we must warn you that the stakes are high, because hell is forever. Every second that you sleep on your calling gives the devil more souls for destruction. The price of fulfilling this call is small when compared to an eternity of hell for a lost soul. Everything you need to begin has been prepared for you. The Word says in Romans 10:6-8, the Word is near you, in your mouth and in your heart.

Uniting The World In Prayer

John 17:21
That they all may be one; as thou, Father, art in me, and I in thee, that they also may be one in us: that the world may believe that thou hast sent me.

When Jesus made this statement He was talking about the Jews and Gentiles coming together as one. At that time there were no Christian denominations, just Jews and Gentiles! Jesus said that this unity would cause the world to know that God sent His Son!

The Jews were given the divine order of worship in the Torah (Tabernacle and the Feasts). However, many do not understand that Jesus is the fulfillment of the shadow pictures in the Torah. On the other hand, many Gentiles have received Christ as the Messiah, but know nothing about their Jewish heritage.

Jesus wants the Jews to understand that He is the Messiah and the fulfillment of the Torah and worship Him in that manner. He also wants Gentiles to take their knowledge of Him as Messiah and apply that to the divine order of worship He gave the Jews. This is the true meaning of the unity Jesus was talking about!

When we unite in this type of worship it will cause the WORLD to know that God sent His Son! Jesus said if we would unite, the same glory that rested upon Him would be upon us! GLORY TO GOD! Praying according to Pattern will accomplish this!

Hidden in the Tabernacle of Moses is the power and ability to unite all in prayer, performing the desires of God's heart. We may all differ in doctrines but if we belong to God and honor His Word we can all come into agreement upon what Jesus accomplished as the fulfillment of the Tabernacle. This gives us a basis for agreement whereby we can come together and worship the Lord in one accord. This will fulfill the following scripture, *"Till we all come in the unity of the faith, and of the knowledge of the Son of God, unto a perfect man, unto the measure of the stature of the fulness of Christ"* (Ephesians 4:13).

It is and always has been God's desire to bring us together as one (John 17:21). One day in prayer, I began to ponder the importance of praying according to Pattern. As the different benefits began to flow across my mind, I heard the Holy Spirit ask, "Have you ever heard of an army that was not organized?" That startled me because the Church is supposed to be the army of God but to date we have no organization! In every army there is government, unification, and specific goals and objectives. With the Tabernacle Prayer Pattern, we can become the mighty army of God. The divine order of the Tabernacle Prayer displays God's government. It also brings unification and by virtue of the declared Word of God establishes His objectives in the earth.

The Tabernacle Prayer Pattern is so unique and multi-faceted that it can be prayed in several different ways. A prayer leader can pray it alone while everyone else comes into agreement. You can also have two people alternate as C.J. and I do, or you can have a group of people, with each person praying a section of the Tabernacle. Another way is to simply follow the leader, with each person adding scriptures applicable to that section. The ultimate level is our desire to bring the Church together, globally, through satellite. We would have each country pray a section of the Tabernacle so that the entire Body of Christ, Jew and Gentile Christians, can come together and worship God as one. When we unify, the glory of God will manifest and the world will know that God sent His Son, the Lord Jesus Christ!

The Vision Of Unity

In 1984, the Lord gave me the invention of a battery-lit torch. I followed through by having my invention copyrighted and later patented as the "Eternal Flame Torch". I tried to market my invention commercially through secular events. Each time I did, I was faced with incredible disappointment and rejection. Every single attempt, and there were many, all failed. What I experienced did not even remotely fit the law of averages! At first, prospective marketers would be absolutely elated with the possibilities and the enormous profits that would ensue, only to turn completely cold the following day.

Frustrated beyond belief, I cried out to the Lord for answers. God told me that my project belonged to Him: and that it would bring the Body of Christ together in worship. He also told me that the Torch was a token of the covenant that He made with Abraham in Genesis 14 and 15. It is symbolic of the fiery torch that passed between the halves of the animals, sealing the covenant. He instructed me to inscribe John 8:12, *"I Am The Light of the World",* on the base of the Torch. At that point I understood that all the rejection was indeed supernatural, it was the Lord Himself blocking those earlier attempts!

He also began to show me a vision of the Body of Christ, globally through satellite coming together, lifting up the Eternal Flame Torch. We were worshipping God as one man, fulfilling

Ephesians 4:13 and John 17:21. I was utterly astounded and overwhelmed, because I was the most unlikely candidate to be the vision-holder of a project of this magnitude.

A few weeks into this new revelation I met C.J. and we both knew instantly that it was a divine appointment. C.J. had been writing prophetic poetry for several years, but did not understand many of them. However in the context of this vision, they were finally understood. In reality, C.J. had been "speaking forth" this vision through her poetry and intercession for years. About a week after hearing the vision, C.J. was given a beautiful poem that captured the heart of the vision and all that God desired to do. The poem is appropriately called *"I Am The Life That Brings The Light!"* God supernaturally put us together and gave us the mandate to pray His vision through to completion. As we began to pray, God gave us the revelation of how it would come to pass. The end result of this vision of "true worship and unity" will be nothing short of worldwide revival, and the long prophesied, end-time harvest of souls!

The Lord, as the Word shows, approaches ordinary people with extraordinary visions. He does not seem to call those that are considered by others to be *"qualified"*. But God chooses to *"qualify"* those that He calls. In 1995, God began this "qualification process" with C.J. and I in the most unique way. We both knew that we had been called as intercessors and teachers. We also knew that God had been preparing us throughout our entire lives for something, but neither of us could foresee what has happened to us. This book is the product of years of daily intercessory prayer, visions, Bible study, fasting, and prophetic words. We began our journey by searching the scriptures for true worshippers. God directed us to the root of correct worship, the Tabernacle of Moses. As we began to diligently study the Tabernacle of Moses, God began to pour out revelation. He then sovereignly taught us to pray according to the divine order within the Tabernacle of Moses.

During this time, C.J. and I experienced great persecution from all quarters. The only way we withstood these attacks was with the Word of God. We have found, as Christians, the only way to fulfill our destiny is to find ourselves in scripture and meditate upon it. The purpose of this is to walk in what has already been written and settled in eternity. When the enemy attacks, meditating upon the Word is the only way to stand and be victorious.

When we stop to think about it, we realize this is exactly what Jesus did. The things that Jesus came to accomplish were written thousands of years before His birth. The first thirty years of His life, He meditated on the scriptures, found Himself in them, and then performed all that was written of Him. The Lord Jesus tells us that He only spoke the words of His Father and only did the works that He saw His Father do. His destiny was to bring into the realm of time that which had been purposed in eternity. We are to also find ourselves in scripture, meditate upon it, and fulfill it.

Yes, your destiny is also written in scripture. Just ask God for it, and He will give it to you. Whether you understand it or not, write it out, stand upon it and He will reveal what He has called you to do. Our mission in this life is to find the will of God and fulfill it.

The first time I asked God to give me a scripture for the Torches I was completely at the end of my rope and was ready to give up. I asked God to give me a scripture so that I would know what to do. The Lord gave me Micah 4:13.

Micah 4:13
Arise and thresh, O daughter of Zion: for I will make thine horn iron, and I will make thy hoofs brass: and thou shalt beat in pieces many people: and I will consecrate their gain unto the LORD, and their substance unto the Lord of the whole earth.

Even though I didn't completely understand it, I wrote it down and began to meditate upon it. It became my strength during those times that I wanted to give up. This scripture actually took seven years for me to truly understand it. *"Arise and thresh"* means to stand up, arise and to break open or thrash the Word of God, as one would remove the chaff from the wheat. It means to literally tear away the hull to receive that which lays hidden inside. The call *"O daughter of Zion"* did not make sense to me at first. But now I know that Zion is the heavenly or spiritual Jerusalem, where we worship the Lord as king-priests and dwell in His presence.

The next sentence states, *"for I will make thine horn iron"*, means that God will make the anointing exceptionally strong. Incidentally, the Hebrew meaning of the word *"horn"* means *"something that projects light"* — that is exactly what the Torch does! Then the next part of this scripture says, *"and I will make thy hoofs brass"*. The word *"hoofs"* surprisingly, means claw, which corresponds to the claw used in the description of Jacob's grappling and wrestling with God (see chapter on Jacob). Brass always symbolizes divine judgment, so God is saying that prayer will go forth with divine judgment. Divine judgment takes place in the Prayer Pattern as we pray the Word of God in divine order and execute the judgment written.

The next section reads, *"and thou shall beat in pieces many people"*, means destroying the strongholds over many nationalities. It also states, *"and I will consecrate their gain unto the LORD and their substance to the Lord of the whole earth"*, which means that their physical and moral being will be consecrated to the Lord of the whole earth. The statement the *"Lord of the whole earth"* means the *"Lord as Conqueror"* and He that rules and reigns over all. The Tabernacle Prayer, with its purging effect, will accomplish this. Many souls will be saved when the prayers of the king-priests of the Lord go forth. God's Word is so deep and as we truly seek we shall find its hidden treasures.

The Lord gave us several other scriptures to stand upon. Two of our favorites were John 17:21 and Isaiah 62:1. John 17:21 states; *"That they all may be one; as thou, Father, art in me, and I in thee, that they also may be one in us: that the world may believe that thou hast sent me"*. Isaiah 62:1 says; *"For Zion's sake I will not hold my peace, and for Jerusalem's sake I will not rest, until the righteousness thereof go forth as brightness, and the salvation thereof as a lamp (Torch) that burneth"*.

There were also many extraordinary experiences relating to this project. The most memorable experience was when C.J. called me late one night and asked if I was sitting down. Thank God I was lying down at the time. Her voice sounded so different I wasn't sure what to expect. Speaking in the voice of eternity, she read to me a section from a book on the Feasts of Israel. At the time, neither of us had studied or had been taught anything about the Feasts of the Lord. We found that two very interesting rituals marked the Feast of Tabernacles. At the height of the Feast, the priest would pour water on the base of the Altar, symbolizing worshipping God for the rain needed for the harvest. Jesus chose this time to tell them that He would provide the rain as rivers of living water that would flow out of their bellies.

John 7:37-39
In the last day, that great day of the Feast, Jesus stood and cried, saying, if any man thirst, let him come unto me, and drink. He that believeth on me, as the scripture hath said, out of his belly shall flow rivers of living water. (But this spake he of the Spirit, which they that believe on him should receive: for the Holy Ghost was not yet given; because that Jesus was not yet glorified.)

In other words, the gift of the Holy Spirit, which was to be given, would bring forth these rivers. The second ritual involved all the Jewish people coming to the Temple area lifting up LIGHTED TORCHES! For miles the lighted torches could be seen all along the countryside. This symbolized worshipping God for the sunshine needed for a successful harvest! Jesus once again tried to let them know that He was the fulfillment of all that the Law of Moses commanded!

John 8:12
Then spake Jesus again unto them, saying, I am the light of the world: he that followeth me shall not walk in darkness, but shall have the light of life.

In essence He was saying, "I Am the Torch", the "Light" that you need for a successful harvest! God not only spoke His vision through scriptures, but He had it reenacted each year in the Feast of Tabernacles! As stated before, the Feasts of Israel correspond to the pattern of the Tabernacle. The Church has already celebrated Passover in the Outer Court and Pentecost in the Holy Place. The Feast of Tabernacles is the last Feast of the year for the Jewish people, but prophetically it is the culmination of the age and the Holy of Holies for the Church. If we, the Body of Christ, come together praying according to Pattern, across the world, it would bring about the most successful harvest of souls ever known to man!

Seeing the magnitude of this vision, we were perplexed as to how this was to be accomplished. We did not doubt, but we were like Mary when told about the impending birth of Jesus, she asked; how is this going to be? The Lord began by showing us exactly what constituted *"true worship"*, which is the unifying element.

During our morning-prayer sessions, God began to show us pieces, as if He were building a house. He was indeed prophetically building the Tabernacle of Moses! God showed Moses the Pattern and furnishings and gave him explicit instructions on how to build them. He also gave Moses the instructions on how to minister unto Him accordingly. Divine order was so important to God, that He told Moses SEVEN TIMES to do everything according to the Pattern that He had shown him. God's approach to man was from the Holy of Holies to the Altar of Sacrifice. Man's approach to God is from the Altar of Sacrifice to the Holy of Holies. As we were praying to God according to Pattern, He began to lay out His eternal plan to us from His approach.

The first thing we learned from the Lord was the vision, the manifested glory of God (Holy of Holies). Then we learned how to get into His Holy presence by worshipping Him in spirit and in truth (Altar of Incense). Then the Lord showed us the most important thing in all of eternity to Him. It is **INTERCESSION FOR LOST SOULS**, so He can have all of His children in eternal fellowship and communion (Table of Shewbread). Then

He revealed to us that the way to bring effective intercession is to become anointed with the Holy Ghost and power (Candlestick). Then we learned that the only way to properly utilize the anointing is to first be washed with the water of the Word (Laver). Finally, God showed us the main ingredient that causes His mercy to work on our behalf: the magnificent Blood of Jesus (Altar of Sacrifice). By that time we did not need to be shown how to enter His gates with thanksgiving because we were already praising Him for His manifold wisdom. Hallelujah!

The first thing most people think about when they hear *"pattern",* is either bondage or it must be boring. In praying according to Pattern, we found ourselves catapulted into a new realm of the Spirit, that we never knew existed before. Boring? Never! Ritualistic? Not a chance! We ascend into God's House, by the grace of the Holy Spirit, declaring the LIVING WORD of God! With that combination, it is impossible to become boring or ritualistic.

Praying this Pattern, we began to understand the importance of daily repentance before prayer. Thanksgiving, praise and hallowing His name caused us to count our blessings and to understand His character. We also learned to praise and exalt the Lord Jesus for His shed Blood, receiving a greater revelation of its power. This type of prayer gave us a greater hunger and thirst for revelation knowledge of the Word of God. It also enabled us to find our destiny in the scriptures. We meditated upon the Word and declared it daily. The power and the anointing of the Holy Ghost were revealed to us in a new dimension. We found the joy of interceding for those that are on the Father's heart. We gained God's heart for **ALL** of the unsaved, and a worldwide mentality not limited to our immediate surroundings. We experienced a revelation of true worship and began to have sweet intimate fellowship with God the Father as "Daddy God", Abba Father.

The Lord also began to show us the importance of worshipping in the Pattern of David. This is warfare praise and worship that includes dancing and singing in the Spirit, which silences the enemy (Psalms 8:2). When we combine prayer in the Pattern of the Tabernacle of Moses and the Davidic order of worship, we will produce the glory of the Temple of Solomon with all the power, glory, anointing, wisdom and wealth. Our God is a good God!

In summary, we realized our holy calling as king-priests unto the Lord and His desire for all to walk in their king-priest ministry. There are some that teach the Tabernacle of Moses, but very few teach it as a daily *"Prayer Pattern"*. There is so much transforming power in this type of prayer. We become true worshippers that produce a worship cloud for the former and latter rain to bring in the end-time harvest of souls.

God spoke the end and then walked us through to the beginning, to show us how it would come to pass. It is our king-priest ministry that will bring about the manifested glory of the presence of God. It will be our unity that will cause the whole earth to be filled with His glory. This is the final rest of the Lord, the Holy of Holies. But we have to start at the front gate and follow divine order to achieve what God has already purposed in eternity!

Num 14:21
But as truly as I live, all the earth shall be filled with the glory of the LORD

The Vision Of Unity!

I Am The "Life" That Brings The "Light"!

While darkness is covering the earth and the people that is true;
The "Light" will chase the darkness completely from view.
The darkness will disappear; it has to leave that's right;
Says The Eternal God; "I Am the 'Life' that brings the 'Light'!"

Jesus is the Light of the world; to follow Him decide;
The "Light of Life" will cover you; in Him you shall abide.
Hear My voice; I declare unto you, arise and shine;
For the glory upon you will show the world that you are Mine.

The brightness of the King of kings, I want to be seen upon you;
And the people will be drawn to Me, if you let My glory shine through.
Throughout the whole earth; I say, My glory you will see;
And the souls that are affected, for all eternity.

From the earth, the face of darkness; it shall be ripped apart;
You shall see and be radiant, and joy will swell your heart.
Praise, honor, and glory will be given unto Me;
For I will turn to you the people; the abundance of the sea.

Lift up your eyes, and you will see that from all around they come;
They gather together in one accord to receive Christ Jesus the Son.
The Blood of Jesus Christ will cleanse all who come, from sin;
With the purifying fire, of the Spirit of God within.

Yes, darkness is covering the earth and the people that is true;
But remember, the "Light" will chase the darkness completely from view.
The darkness will disappear; it has to leave that's right;
Says The Eternal God; "I Am the 'Life' that brings the 'Light'!"

*For Zion's sake will I not hold my peace, and for Jerusalem's
sake I will not rest, until the righteousness thereof
go forth as brightness, and the salvation
thereof as a lamp that burneth.*
Isa 62:1

Chapter Five

The Abrahamic Covenant

In this section you will learn the true meaning of the Covenant of Abraham. We have been taught that it is a covenant of blessing—and it is. But it also has a greater and a more profound meaning that has been hidden until now. In this study of the Abrahamic Covenant, you will discover that it is a "holy covenant" to make us kings and priests unto God!

After reading this section you will know beyond a shadow of a doubt that you have a royal priesthood awaiting your reception. You will also know that this book was not given to tickle your intellect. It is a divine wake up call that will bring the paradigm shift needed to manifest the presence of God. Your royal priesthood is not a metaphor, nor is it a theory. It is literally the desired destiny of the Father for each of us. James 5:7 tells us that *"the husbandman waiteth for the precious fruit of the earth".* We are so glad that He added *"and hath long patience for it!"* Let's not keep Him waiting any longer.

Melchizedek

If you ask most Christians where their covenant is located in the Bible they would tell you Genesis 12. As glorious as that portion of scripture is, it is an account of the promises and not the actual covenant. In the Old Testament most covenants contained a meal, an oath, and a blood sacrifice or the mingling of blood. These elements are found in Genesis 14 and 15. Let's begin our study in Genesis 14:18-20.

Gen 14:18-20
And Melchizedek KING of Salem brought forth bread and wine: and he was the PRIEST of the most high God. And he blessed him, and said, Blessed be Abram of the most high God, possessor of heaven and earth: And blessed be the most high God, which hath delivered thine enemies into thy hand. And he gave him tithes of all.

The first major point to note is that Melchizedek was a KING AND A PRIEST. The second major point is that no one else in the entire Bible was ever described as being the priest of the Most High God. Even Moses, a man dear to God, with whom He spoke to face to face, was never described in that manner. The rule of *"first mention"* is always very significant, but the title *"THE PRIEST OF THE MOST HIGH GOD"* holds first, last and only mention! To get a clearer understanding of who Melchizedek really was, let's go to the book of Hebrews, the seventh chapter.

Heb 7:1-3
For this Melchisedec, king of Salem, priest of the most high God, who met Abraham returning from the slaughter of the kings, and blessed him; To whom also Abraham gave a tenth part of all; first being by interpretation King of righteousness, and after that also King of Salem, which is, King of peace; Without father, without mother, without descent, having neither beginning of days, nor end of life; but made like unto the Son of God; ABIDETH A PRIEST CONTINUALLY.

God has given us powerful clues regarding the importance of Melchizedek. He begins by emphasizing the subject stating *"this Melchizedec"*. He interprets the name and also tells us to consider how great this man was. Additionally, He presents us with the most spectacular description that can only be compared to the Godhead. No human has a resume like this: without father or mother, having neither beginning of days nor end of life, but made LIKE UNTO THE SON OF GOD; ABIDETH A PRIEST CONTINUALLY. Furthermore, the interpretation of his name means *"King of righteousness"*, *"King of Salem, which is, King of peace"*. It is not only capitalized giving great honor, but it is beyond human capacity! The highest title a human king ever attained was to be king over a geographical area or nation of people, never a characteristic of the Almighty God! Melchizedek was the HOLY GHOST!

Before we continue to bring forth this revelation, it is necessary to follow the word through to its root meaning. This can mean following a chain of references that would be too cumbersome to list. We suggest you take the time to study this in a Bible Concordance on your own; the full interpretation will bless you tremendously and increase your revelation. But for this book, we will highlight and paraphrase the interpretations.

In the Greek, Melchizedek means a Patriarch. A patriarch is a father, the male leader of a family or tribe as in Abraham, Isaac, and Jacob. It is someone regarded as the founder or original head of an enterprise, organization, or tradition. It is also one who is a high dignitary of the priesthood empowered to invoke blessings.

In the Hebrew, Melchizedek means, one who has the power to bring righteousness, make right, make amends, cleanse and to justify. His name also denotes a royal king that has the power to ascend the throne and induct into royalty, and set up or make kings and queens. He is someone who bestows the natural, moral or legal right to have prosperity. Melchizedek was also the King of Salem. Salem means peace, perfected, whole, prosperous, restore, and reward.

This Melchizedek came to make us kings and priests unto God. He also came to bless us with righteousness, wholeness, peace, and prosperity! Another important point to consider is that Melchizedek belonged to *"another tribe"* (Hebrews 7:13). The priesthood of Melchizedek and Jesus Christ came from a different tribe, which was from heaven not earth. God, not man, gave their priesthood to them with an oath.

Heb 7:21
For those priests were made without an oath; but this with an oath by him that said unto him, The Lord sware and will not repent, Thou art a priest for ever after THE ORDER OF MELCHISEDEC:

Now that we understand Melchizedek was the Holy Ghost lets continue to learn what took place.

Gen 14:18-19
And Melchizedek king of Salem brought forth BREAD AND WINE: and he was the priest of the most high God. And he BLESSED him, and said, BLESSED be Abram of the most high God, possessor of heaven and earth:

Our definition of the word *"blessed"* is nothing like the Hebrew definition. This word is so interesting it will astound you to know all that pertains to it. *"Bless"* means to kneel; to bless God as an act of adoration, and vice-versa; man as a benefit. It also means to abundantly bless, congratulate, kneel, praise, salute and to thank. Furthermore, it means by euphemism to curse god or the king, as treason.

At first when I read this, all I could see were the words *"to curse god or the king as treason"*. I thought I had totally missed it! This can't be true because the Holy Spirit would not have anything to do with cursing God or treason. God asked me; *"who is the god of this world?"* When I answered that satan is, I began to see the logic. Melchizedek, in a covert operation, came to officiate a holy covenant with Abraham to destroy the god of this world and to take back all that he has stolen from man. What a powerful word! That quickly settled the matter and I moved on to see the powerful meaning within this definition. Abraham knelt as an act of adoration and worship. The phrases *"vice-versa and man as a benefit"*, tells us there were two-way blessings being given. God was blessing Abraham and he was blessing God. Each party was declaring their covenant promises!

Next we have Melchizedek declaring that Abraham is blessed of the Most High God, possessor of heaven and earth. That means Abraham was blessed with spiritual and physical blessings. Then he declared blessed be God, which has delivered Abraham's enemies into his hand. Not only was a covenant being made to bless Abraham but there was also a covenant being made to destroy his enemies. The word *"euphemism"* in the explanation of *"bless"*, means to substitute a mild word for one considered offensive. For example Melchizedek, declaring that all Abraham's enemies would be placed in his hand was a mild way of saying that God was going to annihilate every one of them! There was two-fold power being released in this covenant, one to bless Abraham the other to destroy the god of this world!

This definition of the word *"blessed"* leaves our previous understanding of that word far behind. Actually to bless means we declare covenant words to God in worship and He declares and releases His covenant blessings upon us. Praying in the pattern of the Tabernacle is a perfect way to accomplish this. We declare and decree His Word as king-priests and Jesus, our High Priest, decrees and confers covenant blessings upon us thereby destroying our enemies. For example: declaring that by His stripes we are healed, Jesus confirms that Word and sends forth the healing and of course when He does all spirits of infirmity are defeated!

The Bread And Wine From Heaven

Gen 14:18
And Melchizedek king of Salem brought forth bread and wine: and he was the priest of the most high God.

Melchizedek was not bringing food for Abraham, but Holy Communion elements to cut covenant. In order to understand this holy covenant, we must know the true meaning of the bread and the wine. Jesus said in Matthew 26:28, the wine they drank in communion was the Blood He shed for the remission of sins. The Hebrew definition of *"bread"* takes us through six references and its complete meaning is amazing! It begins by calling it food, bread, shewbread, also the grain for making it. The Hebrew definition of *"bread"* means to war, battle, prevail, overcome and be delivered. It also means to **BUILD THE FAMILY AND THE HOUSE OF GOD!** In the Greek it means to forgive sin, remove and take away. Clearly this describes our Lord and Savior Jesus Christ-the Bread from Heaven! He is the only one that can bring deliverance, give us the power to overcome our enemies and to build the House of God.

The most important and glorious aspect of this covenant is the fact that it is completely impossible for it to fail! Melchizedek brought down the *"Bread from Heaven"*, which is symbolic of Jesus, and fed it to Abraham and then cut covenant! It cannot fail because God cut the covenant with JESUS CHRIST IN ABRAHAM!

Gal 3:16
Now to Abraham and his seed were the promises made. He saith not, And to seeds, as of many; but as of one, And to thy seed, which is Christ.

God cut covenant with Jesus Christ, the *"Living Bread"*, Whom He knew would not break the covenant. Abraham could have blown it, but not Jesus! Now we can fully understand the Hebrew definition of the *"bread"*. Jesus is our nourishment strength and power to do battle, prevail and overcome every foe within and without. He is the "Children's Bread of Deliverance!" Without a doubt, it was Jesus Christ with Whom the covenant was made and relied upon.

John 6:32-33
Then Jesus said unto them, Verily, verily, I say unto you,
Moses gave you not that bread from heaven; but my Father
giveth you the true bread from heaven. For the bread of
God is he which cometh down from heaven, and giveth life
unto the world.

God temporarily lost the world to satan through Adam. Do you really think He was going to put our entire existence totally upon the shoulders of fallen man? NO! Praise God for His manifold wisdom, because we see in Genesis 16 that Abraham began to go astray by not adhering to the covenant promise that Sarah would have a child. That's why God swore by Himself, to bring this covenant to pass and **HE DID; HE SWORE BY JESUS!**

Heb 6:13-14
For when God made promise to Abraham, because he could
swear by no greater, he sware by himself, Saying, surely
blessing I will bless thee, and multiplying I will multiply
thee.

This was a holy covenant that involved the entire Godhead! Melchizedek, the Holy Spirit, brought Jesus the Bread and Wine from heaven and God the Father sealed the covenant with an oath! All God needed from Abraham was his faith, to believe Him. He did not need his brilliance or his strength. It is exactly the same today. All God needs is our faith in Him and His Word and He will do the rest!

The covenant was made with Jesus Christ, Who lives within you. If you do your part of the covenant, **IT WILL BE IMPOSSIBLE FOR YOU TO FAIL OR LOSE.** You have the awesome power of the King of Glory inside of you, backed by a sworn oath from Almighty God and total guidance from the

Holy Spirit! All you have to do is bless the Lord by speaking covenant words to Him according to Pattern. Let God arise and His enemies be scattered. Hallelujah! The only hope the devil had was to keep us in the dark about our true covenant. He didn't want us to know that we are king-priests blessed of the Most High God, anointed to destroy his works and to possess this earth for the glory of God!

The Cutting Of The Covenant

Gen 15:9-10
And he said unto him, Take me an HEIFER of three years old, and a SHE GOAT of three years old, and a RAM of three years old, and a TURTLE DOVE, and a YOUNG PIGEON. And he took unto him all these, and divided them in the midst, and laid each piece one against another: but the BIRDS divided he not.

Gen 15:17-18
And it came to pass, that, when the sun went down, and it was dark, behold a SMOKING FURNACE, AND A BURNING LAMP that passed between those pieces. In the same day the LORD made a covenant with Abram, saying, Unto thy seed have I given this land, from the river of Egypt unto the great river, the river Euphrates:

God told Abraham to gather particular elements for the actual cutting of the covenant. Notice verse 10 says, that he took them and divided them in the midst and laid each piece one against another; but the birds were not divided. Prophetically God is saying that He had the heifer, the she-goat, and the ram divided in half and placed them against one another because all of these elements represent our desperate need for Jesus. We cannot be perfected without Jesus, the *"Smoking Furnace and Burning Lamp"*, coming in the midst of us.

Yet the turtledove, symbolic of the Holy Spirit, was not divided because God has purposed for us to walk in the full power of the Holy Spirit. The young pigeon had no feathers, due to the fact that his feathers were plucked and stripped off. Therefore it was symbolic of us losing our *"coats of glory"* through Adam's sin. It also was not divided because God has declared that we will recover all that the devil has stolen from us. We will recover our glory, wealth, and dominion, not half but ALL! Glory to the only wise God for His blessed covenant!

We must believe the Word of God to the point, that absolutely nothing will make us doubt it. We are to win the nations and we are not going to do it powerless and broke. Nor will it happen by osmosis! We must take up our king-priest duties, declare and war for it according to Pattern. We must uproot every lie of the enemy that speaks against our covenant right to be anointed, wealthy, and victorious over the devil. Many people are dying and going to hell because we, the Body of Christ, are not showing the world the power of the gospel. It is time to become the king-priests that God has called us to be. We are destined to be the anointed, wealthy, victorious Church that Jesus so lovingly laid down His life to create.

Chapter Six

Jacob

Lev 26:40-42
If they shall confess their iniquity, and the iniquity of their fathers, with their trespass which they trespassed against me, and that also they have walked contrary unto me; And that I also have walked contrary unto them, and have brought them into the land of their enemies; if then their uncircumcised hearts be humbled, and they then accept of the punishment of their iniquity: Then will I remember my covenant with Jacob, and also my covenant with Isaac, and also my covenant with Abraham will I remember; and I will remember the land.

Clearly stated in these scriptures, if we repent for our sins and the sins of our fathers God will remember the covenants of Jacob, Isaac and Abraham. Not only is God speaking to us through the meanings of each of these covenants, He is also prophetically giving us a message in the order that He chose to present them. Out of the several references to the covenants of Abraham, Isaac and Jacob this is the first and only time it was placed in the reverse order.

We believe these three covenants were compounded to bless us abundantly. However, the reverse order shows the importance of Jacob who is a prophetic archetype of a mighty king-priest intercessor. You will see in the following pages that this type of intercessor produces the kind of repentance that God needs to forgive our sins and heal our land.

The covenant of Jacob is our covenant of transformation and intercession to bring about the desire of the Father's heart and His end-time purposes in the earth. The covenant of Isaac shows us, as we become living sacrifices, holy and acceptable unto God, He will become our God of miracles. And the covenant promise of Abraham was made to the "Seed", the Lord Jesus Christ, Who made us kings and priests by His Blood. In this case God was speaking the *"end from the beginning"* in showing us the *"archetype of transformation"* that will produce His end-time glory in the earth!

To embark upon this wonderful journey into transforming our lives and the entire Body of Christ, let's look at Genesis 25:23-26, where the Lord told Rebekah that she would have twins and the elder would serve the younger.

Gen 25:23-26
And the LORD said unto her, Two nations are in thy womb, and two manner of people shall be separated from thy bowels; and the one people shall be stronger than the other people; and the ELDER SHALL SERVE THE YOUNGER. And when her days to be delivered were fulfilled, behold, there were twins in her womb. And the first came out red, all over like an hairy garment; and they called his name Esau. And after that came his brother out, AND HIS HAND TOOK HOLD ON ESAU'S HEEL; and his name was called Jacob: and Isaac was threescore years old when she bare them.

"Esau" was the elder and his name in the Hebrew means in essence, handling something rough that should have been sensibly felt. As we can see in Genesis 25:30-34, Esau did not handle things sensibly. Esau sold his birthright to Jacob for one morsel of meat (Hebrews 12:16). Esau may have been hungry but not nearly desperate enough to sell his birthright. That is why it was commented in Genesis 25:34, *"thus Esau despised his birthright"*, because after he ate and drank he was on his way without so much as a second thought as to what had just happened.

Jacob, on the other hand, was well acquainted with the covenant God made with his grandfather and reaffirmed with his father. He understood that possessing the birthright meant that his bloodline would be the channel through which the covenant would be accomplished. His heart burned with the desire to fulfill that destiny.

However, the most misunderstood and controversial action in the life of Jacob occurred when his mother (fulfilling the prophecy) helped him to obtain the blessing of the firstborn by pretending to be Esau (Genesis 27:15-19).

Gen 27:41
And Esau hated Jacob because of the blessing wherewith his father blessed him: and Esau said in his heart, The days of mourning for my father are at hand; then will I slay my brother Jacob.

At first, when we look at this in the natural, all we can see is deceit and trickery. But let's look at it from another perspective. Esau, who not only sold his birthright to Jacob for food, married two Canaanite women who were idol worshippers. These marriages grieved his parents because they knew it was important to marry within their kindred. Abraham made his servant swear by an oath not to get a wife for Isaac from the Canaanites, but go to his country and kindred. Likewise Esau should have also received a wife from his own country and kindred. But Esau married these women anyway bringing grief upon his parents. It is conceivable that when God had spoken to Rebekah (Genesis 25:23), saying that the elder shall serve the younger, that Isaac was well aware of this prophecy. However, because he favored Esau over Jacob, he was going to go against the Word of the Lord! What is interesting to note is the fact that Isaac was blind, and as we conclude from the scriptures, almost at the point of death. Yet we find that he lived many years after this incident.

Could the blindness and apparent sickness be contributed to the fact he was in rebellion to the will of God concerning giving Jacob the blessing? In addition there had to be a supernatural blindness over Isaac to pull this off. God's ways are not our ways and sometimes God goes to what we believe are *"questionable measures"* to bring about His will. There is a lot more to Jacob than what we have previously discerned and it is time for us to see the truth in the life of Jacob.

Up until this time, we have looked at Jacob as a deceiver, but that is not how God saw him! Jacob is called in Deuteronomy 32:10, the apple of God's eye! God also calls Himself the *"Mighty God of Jacob"*. There is much more to Jacob than we can see in the natural, but by the time you finish this section you will know why God is the proud Father of Jacob.

The House Of God

After Jacob received the birthright blessings from his father, Esau threatened to kill him. When Rebekah learned of the threats she advised Jacob to leave and go to her brother Laban's house in Haran. On the way to Haran, Jacob had a visitation from God, which is profound and awesome in scope.

Gen 28:12-17
AND HE DREAMED, AND BEHOLD A LADDER SET UP ON THE EARTH, AND THE TOP OF IT REACHED TO HEAVEN: AND BEHOLD THE ANGELS OF GOD ASCENDING AND DESCENDING ON IT. And, behold, the LORD stood above it, and said, I am the LORD God of Abraham thy father, and the God of Isaac: the land whereon thou liest, to thee will I give it, and to thy seed; And thy seed shall be as the dust of the earth, and thou shalt spread abroad to the west, and to the east, and to the north, and to the south: and in thee and in thy seed shall all the families of the earth be blessed. And, behold, I am with thee, and will keep thee in all places whither thou goest, and will bring thee again into this land; for I will not leave thee, until I have done that which I have spoken to thee of. And Jacob awaked out of his sleep, and he said, Surely the LORD is in this place; and I knew it not. And he was afraid, and said, How dreadful is this place! this is none other but the HOUSE OF GOD, AND THIS IS THE GATE OF HEAVEN.

The interpretation of this dream is the key to the transformation and perfecting of the Saints and the glorification of the Church. The first thing to grasp from the metaphor of the ladder is that it is symbolic of Jesus, Who is the Way, THE ONLY WAY TO GOD! Secondly, the ladder connects heaven and earth. Jesus is the only mediator between heaven and earth. Thirdly the ladder, with its steps, signifies that there are divine steps to enter into God's presence.

Speaking the Word of God in divine order, as illustrated in the Tabernacle Prayer, is parallel to ascending the steps of the ladder into the presence of God. This type of prayer is the only process by which angels ascend and descend on our behalf. According to Psalms 103:20, angels heed only the voice of the Word of God, not our cries or opinions.

The statement Jacob made in Genesis 28:17, *"How dreadful is this place!"* signifies the awesome power that is available in the House of God. Jacob also said, *"this is none other than the house of God, and this is the gate of heaven"*. Jesus said in Luke 19:46 that His house is the house of prayer.

Praying according to the Pattern of the House of God gives us the power to go through the gate, and up to the *"High Places"*. In the High Places spiritual warfare is accomplished more easily and effectively. In this realm we are seated with Christ in heavenly places, far above all the power of the enemy (Ephesians 1:20-21).

Gen 28:18-19
And Jacob rose up early in the morning, and took the STONE that he had put for his pillows, and set it up for a pillar, and poured oil upon the top of it. And he called the name of that place BETHEL: but the name of that city was called LUZ at the first.

I Peter 2:6
Wherefore also it is contained in the scripture, Behold, I lay in Sion a CHIEF CORNER STONE, elect, precious: and he that believeth on him shall not be confounded.

The stone Jacob anointed was a memorial stone for the House of God. That stone is symbolic of none other than the Chief Corner Stone of the House of God, Jesus Christ. *"Bethel"* means the House of God. Incredibly, the chain of references also takes us to the same word for ram, which was an element in the covenant of Abraham. The ram means having the strength of Almighty God.

Therefore, Bethel or the House of God will give us the power to have the strength of the Almighty within us. *"Luz"* in the Hebrew means an almond tree, which prophetically means revelation knowledge and being completely awake spiritually. Praying the divine steps of the House of God will bring us into wisdom, understanding, revelation knowledge, and power as we ascend into the presence of God.

In this dream Jacob saw angels ascending and descending the ladder. They are God's emissaries on the earth, sent to minister for the heirs of salvation. They only hearken to the voice of the Word of God. They ascend the ladder of the House of God with our prayers spoken in divine order and descend to bring the manifestation to the earth realm. Jacob had a powerful revelation concerning the House of God being the House of Prayer. As we ascend into the House of God according to the Pattern (steps), we will be able to bring the eternal purposes of God into the physical realm!

The Transformation

Right after Jacob experienced this magnificent dream, he vowed a very interesting vow.

Gen 28:20-22
And Jacob vowed a vow, saying, If God will be with me, and will keep me IN THIS WAY that I go, and will give me BREAD TO EAT, and RAIMENT to put on, So that I come again to my father's house in PEACE; then shall the LORD

be my God: And this stone, which I have set for a pillar, shall be God's house: and of all that thou shalt give me I will surely give the tenth unto thee.

We, the New Testament Church, should know and understand this vow. Jacob is asking God to keep him in the path of righteousness. He also asks for provision in the form of bread and clothing. He then asks for the peace of God to restore him to his family. Further studies of the key words in this passage reveal some hidden truths. When Jacob saw the ladder and angels ascending and descending, he knew that he was privileged to see how the Kingdom of God operates. He then asks to be kept in *"this way"*, the way of righteousness where angelic power is available. As revealed earlier, the *"bread"* represents the ability to war, to do battle, prevail and overcome. When Jacob asks for bread, he was in essence, asking for deliverance and the power to overcome all things.

The word *"raiment"* means a covering for unfaithfulness, deceit, and transgressions. This was Jacob's prayer of repentance; he was asking God for a covering for his sins. He also asked to be brought back to his father's house in peace. *"Peace"* in the Hebrew is the word *"shalom"* which means peace, prosperity, wealth, wholeness, and soundness. Jacob was asking God for total deliverance with favor and blessings.

Jacob's vow has a prophetic significance for us. We are to walk in the revelation of *"the way"* the Kingdom of God operates, which is praying according to Pattern so that angelic power is available. We are to receive the *"Bread of Life"*, which is Jesus Christ, the *"Children's Bread of Deliverance"* to overcome all things. The Holy Ghost is our *"raiment"*, covering our sin nature, so that we can return to God our Father in *"peace"* with total restoration.

This dream had a profound effect upon Jacob. This can be seen in his reaction to what took place in his life over the next twenty years.

Gen 31:41
Thus have I been twenty years in thy house; I served thee fourteen years for thy two daughters, and six years for thy cattle: and thou has changed my wages ten times.

Jacob's new life and walk with God was thoroughly tested by Laban and found complete. If Jacob had not changed he would not have been able to endure this test. Jacob endured until God told him to leave and return to his homeland. As Jacob approached his homeland, he sent messengers before him to Esau his brother. He sent with them a peace offering so that he might find favor. The messengers returned to Jacob and told him that Esau was coming to meet him with four hundred men and he was afraid (Genesis 32:6-7). After prayer, Jacob positioned his people across the brook and he returned to the camp and slept alone.

Wrestling With God

Gen 32:24-30
And Jacob was left alone; and there wrestled a man with him until the breaking of the day. And when he saw that he prevailed not against him, he touched the hollow of his thigh; AND THE HOLLOW OF JACOB'S THIGH WAS OUT OF JOINT, AS HE WRESTLED WITH HIM. And he said, Let me go, for the day breaketh. And he said, I will not let thee go, EXCEPT THOU BLESS ME. And he said unto him, What is thy name? And he said, Jacob. And he said, THY NAME SHALL BE CALLED NO MORE JACOB, BUT ISRAEL: FOR AS A PRINCE HAST THOU POWER WITH GOD AND WITH MEN, AND HAST PREVAILED. And Jacob asked him, and said, Tell me, I pray thee, thy name. And he said, Wherefore is it that thou dost ask after my name? AND HE BLESSED

HIM THERE. And Jacob called the name of the place Pe-ni'-el: for I have seen God face to face, and my life is preserved.

It is quite easy to see why God loved Jacob. Not only did he wrestle all night long through the darkest hours, but he would not stop even though his hip had been knocked out of place. The Word says, *"his thigh was out of joint 'AS' he wrestled"*. The man wrestling with him had to ask Jacob to let him go! Jacob had such a great desire for the blessings of God that he became relentless in his pursuit. Jacob proved to God just how much he wanted the covenant blessings, by refusing to let go until he had been blessed.

The man asked Jacob for his name; he then *"blessed"* Jacob by changing his name to *"Israel"*. Then we see Jacob asking the man for his name, so he could bless him also. Jacob wanted to enter into a two-way blessing denoting a covenant relationship. Then the scripture states that the man asked Jacob why he asked for his name: and the man *"blessed"* Jacob. This word *"blessed"* is different from the first reference. This word means that God *"blessed"* Jacob by being straight, on the level, and honest — MEANING THAT HE REVEALED WHO HE REALLY WAS!

The next scripture confirms this, Jacob named the place Peniel because he had seen God face-to-face and lived! There should be no doubt that Jacob encountered the Lord Himself. The word *"wrestle"* in the Hebrew surprisingly means to float away as a vapor. It means to seize or hold as with a grapple. The word *"grapple"* means an iron claw for grasping and holding something alongside. Here we have vapors rising as we have an iron clad hold upon God.

To *"wrestle"* is a perfect example of prayer and the essence of Praying in the Pattern of the Tabernacle! As explained earlier in the section on the *"Former and Latter Rain"*, prayer according to Pattern produces vapors that ascend into heaven. Releasing pleasing vapors of worship unto the Father can only come from intercessors grappling with God—praying the Word of God.

When we pray according to Pattern, we have an iron clad grasp upon the Lord because He is the fulfillment of every step in the Tabernacle! Jacob wrestling with God is a prophetic snapshot of the perfect way to pray. The word *"prevail"* in Genesis 32:28 means to attain, overcome, have power, and to stop. This type of prayer gives us the power, literally to receive and attain converts for the Kingdom of God! It also helps us to overcome the works of the devil, and have power to stop the enemy from destroying the people of God!

Genesis 32:25 states that *"he touched the hollow of his thigh"*. The word *"touch"* means to bring down, strike, and plague. The word *"hollow"* means power, also to bow down self. The word *"thigh"* means the generative parts, to produce or to procreate offspring. The word *"joint"* means to sever oneself, be alienated and out of joint.

Let's combine everything to get a prophetic picture of what God is saying to us. We will have the power to pray for and produce a Godly offspring from those who have been beaten, brought down, and plagued. There is power in Jacob to pray and affect the people that have been alienated, dislocated and severed themselves from God! The next scriptures will shed more light on the power that is hidden in Jacob.

Gen 32:31
And as he passed over Pen-nu-el the sun rose upon him, and he HALTED upon his thigh.

The word *"halted"* means to limp as if one-sided. Jacob became one-sided upon his generative parts, or his ability to produce and procreate. If you really look back over Jacob's life you will find this is true. Throughout his entire life, he was completely focused and concerned about obtaining the covenant blessings and perpetuating them in his children.

Let's continue with verse 32 to complete this prophetic picture of the perfect intercessor.

Gen 32:32
Therefore the children of Israel eat not of the sinew which shrank, which is upon the hollow of the thigh, unto this day: because he touched the hollow of Jacob's thigh in THE SINEW THAT SHRANK.

The word *"sinew"* means a thong. A thong means, a leather strip for binding and lashing. The word *"sinew"* also means to attack, invade, overcome and assemble troops. The word *"shrank"* means a sense of failure, crippled, deprive, remove and to forget. Prophetically, God is saying that Jacob has the power to bind, lash, and overcome the enemy. Jacob will assemble the army of God, and remove their sense of failure, inability and deprivation! The manifold wisdom of God is awesome! Within Jacob is the true power of spiritual warfare!

No wonder God states that Jacob is His inheritance and the apple of His eye. When we come to the full understanding of the truth of Jacob, we will become that mighty army that God has sent His Son to achieve. Spiritually, Jacob became one-sided upon binding and overcoming the enemy and gathering the army of God. He was also one-sided upon reaching the lost, the failed, the crippled, the forgotten, and the deprived. Wrestling with God, which is praying according to Pattern, will give you a heart for lost souls and the army of God!

Jacob was a man who reverenced God all of his life. From birth he had a strong desire for the things of God. In reality, there wasn't any form of rebellion or irreverence of God recorded in the life of Jacob. If Jacob were out of the will of God concerning the birthright blessings, God would have told him. He never passed up the opportunity to tell Saul of his wrong doings, neither was He beyond telling David and countless others of His displeasure. Yet God never addressed Jacob because it was prophesied before his birth that the elder shall serve the younger.

Primarily the Church has seen Jacob as a trickster and a supplanter, yet Jacob produced the chosen people of God. Likewise, when we become the king-priests of the House of God, we will also produce the chosen people of God. What awesome power and responsibility has been entrusted to us! Jacob's life is a metaphor showing that prayer according to the divine order of the House of God will bring forth the power and the glory to redeem and transform His people!

The Heel Catcher

The name *"Jacob"* means heel catcher, supplanter, and patriarch. It also means to seize by the heel, circumvent by tripping up the heels and to supplant. Furthermore, Jacob denotes the rear of an army, a lier in wait. The word *"lier"* is an old French word meaning to bind and it reaffirms the importance of binding in prayer.

Let's examine the word *"heel"*. That word appears only six times in the Bible. The first time it appears God is pronouncing judgment upon satan in the Garden of Eden.

Gen 3:15
And I will put enmity between thee and the woman, and between thy seed and her seed; it shall bruise thy head, and thou shalt bruise his HEEL.

The next time the word *"heel"* is used Jacob has a hold of Esau's heel. The next four references depict the heel as something that was against another. There is only one reference to the heel in the New Testament and that is attributed to Judas Iscariot.

John 13:18
I speak not of you all: I know whom I have chosen: but that the scripture may be fulfilled, He that eateth bread with me hath lifted up his HEEL against me.

Judas was also classified as the son of perdition (John 17:12). Perdition means ruin or loss. It also means to be physically, spiritually or eternally damnable. Now let's revisit Genesis 3:15. God told satan in the garden that He, Jesus, would crush his head, and he, satan, shall bruise His heel.

The headship and authority of satan was crushed when Jesus arose victoriously from the grave. The prophecy that he shall bruise Jesus' heel means that there will be some people who, no matter what you do, will choose to go the way of perdition. But the end-time intercessors of Jacob, praying according to Pattern, are going to be the *"HEEL CATCHERS"* to stop as many as possible from going into perdition!

Jacob is the end-time army that has the power with God and with men through intercession. We, as king-priests unto God, have the power to stop the destruction against God's people. This is accomplished by washing their feet with the Word of God. Jesus gave us a powerful example concerning this in the following scripture.

John 13:14
If I then, your Lord and Master, have washed your feet; ye also ought to wash one another's feet. For I have given you an example, that ye should do as I have done to you.

The disciples were literally washed with the water by the Word! This is exactly what we need to do to our fellow man. We need to wash their feet, which is their walk, with the water of the Word of God. We are to become *"HEEL CATCHERS"* by washing one another's feet with the water of the Word of God in prayer. We are also to pray for all men that they will not be victims of perdition but turn to God for salvation and strength.

The word *"supplanter"*, also attributed to the name of Jacob, can be looked at from a very positive perspective. Supplant means to displace, unseat and to succeed. Jacob, as supplanter, has the power to displace, unseat and succeed over the god of this world, satan!

Jacob is a mighty archetype that will supplant the god of this world, assemble the mighty army of God, and redeem as many as possible from the enemy. In Jacob, is the power to bring in the end-time harvest of souls and to perfect the Saints for the Glory of God!

Chapter Seven

The Patriarchs

God gave each patriarch, Abraham, Isaac, Jacob, Moses, David and Solomon a part of laying the foundation for our king-priest ministry. By studying the Patriarchs we will clearly see how God has used each one to build the way for us to fulfill our destiny to become the manifested sons of God.

Abraham

Abraham entered into a holy covenant with God to make us kings and priests and he sacrificed his son. This covenant sacrifice provided the way for Jesus Christ, the Chief Cornerstone and Foundation of the House of God, to come forth. Yes, covenant love made the way for God to manifest His Son in the earth and sacrifice Him for the sins of the world. We, as New Testament king-priests, must offer our Father the sacrifice of praise in order to manifest Jesus in our lives!

Isaac

Isaac was Abraham's miracle child and the son that he sacrificed at God's direction. And we know God accepted the fact that Abraham had sacrificed Isaac in his heart, therefore He did not require his physical death. Isaac is the type of the *"living sacrifice"* and we are told to present our bodies as living sacrifices unto the Lord as our reasonable *"worship"* (Romans 12:1). Therefore, we are to die to ourselves and to worship God in the manner in which He requires.

Jacob

Jacob received a prophetic dream that revealed the purpose for the House of God, to be the House of Prayer. Jacob's dream also reveals that prayer offered in divine order, as shown by the steps of the ladder, takes us into the presence of God and summons angelic power on behalf of all men.

Moses

Moses was given the Torah, which contained the pattern for the Tabernacle, God's dwelling place. It also contained the divine order of worship for the priesthood and the Feasts of the Lord. These truths that Moses received enabled the glory of God to dwell upon the earth. As New Testament king-priests we are to build a spiritual Tabernacle so the glory of God can cover the earth as the waters cover the sea.

David

The Ark of the Covenant was brought to Mount Zion when David entered his king-priest ministry. When we enter our king-priest ministry we will also bring in the presence of God for this end-time revival!

Solomon

Solomon, the man of peace, was a type of the Prince of Peace, the Lord Jesus Christ. He built the Temple of God and worshipped in the divine order of the Tabernacle of Moses and the pattern of worship that David established. The Temple of Solomon, in its entire splendor, is prophetic of the apostolic fullness and glory of the New Testament Church, which is to come!

After briefly reviewing the most important aspects of their lives, we clearly see the correlation between their accomplishments and our holy calling! We serve a wise God!

Chapter Eight

David And Solomon

The Tabernacle Of David

Amos 9:11-12
In that day will I raise up the tabernacle of David that is fallen, and close up the breaches thereof; and I will raise up his ruins, and I will build it as in the days of old: THAT THEY MAY POSSESS THE REMNANT OF EDOM, AND OF ALL THE HEATHEN, WHICH ARE CALLED BY MY NAME, saith the LORD that doeth this.

The main reason that God desires to raise up the Tabernacle of David is so that we may "possess" our inheritance, which are the heathen nations coming to Christ. When we discuss the restoration of the Tabernacle of David, we mean the spiritual significance of restoring the Davidic order of worship. David, as king and priest following divine order, brought the Ark to Mount Zion. As mentioned earlier, the manifested presence of the Lord in the forthcoming revival will be brought in upon the shoulders of the New Testament king-priests.

Mount Zion, where the Ark rested, was a hill in Jerusalem whose ancient name was Hermon. In the Old Testament, the word *"Zion"* means a permanent capital, a monumental guiding pillar, and a goal or something bright at a distance that we should travel towards. Furthermore, it means to be a superintendent of the Temple services and its music. In the New Testament, *"Zion"* means perpetual, constant, strength, victory, and the Church militant and triumphant.

When we combine these definitions, it is obvious that they describe both earthly and heavenly Zion. Earthly Zion was where David set up his king-priest government, which foreshadowed the ministry of Jesus. The Lord Jesus Christ came as a King-Priest after the order of Melchizedek to establish our way into spiritual or heavenly Zion -- into the very presence of God.

Heavenly Zion or heavenly Jerusalem is the city of God according to Hebrews 12:22, and of course it is a permanent guiding pillar, a bright goal that we should travel towards! We travel to spiritual or heavenly Zion by praying in the Pattern of the Tabernacle of Moses and worshipping in the Pattern of the Tabernacle of David. We then come forth as the victorious Church, militant and triumphant! Glory to God!

Another reason why God desires to restore the Tabernacle of David, the Davidic order of worship, is that God wants to restore the perfection of worship to the Church. In the Tabernacle of Moses, only the High Priest once a year had access to the presence of God. While in the Tabernacle of

David, a number of priests had access to the presence of God twenty-four hours a day and there was continuous worship before the unveiled Ark. It is God's desire that we ALL have access to His presence!

Another undeniable factor in Davidic worship is that David had both Tabernacles operating simultaneously. According to I Chronicles 16:39-40, burnt offerings were continually offered morning and evening at the Tabernacle at Gibeon. It also states that they continued to do all that was written in the Law of the Lord. This illustrates that it is important to have the divine order of prayer and approach to God, as in the Tabernacle of Moses, and the divine order of free flowing worship as instituted by David in his Tabernacle. When we pray and worship in this manner, we will manifest the presence of God and bring in the end-time harvest of souls!

Isa 2:2-3
And it shall come to pass in the last days, that the mountain of the LORD's house shall be established in the top of the mountains, and shall be exalted above the hills; and all nations shall flow unto it. And many people shall go and say, Come ye, and let us go up to the mountain of the LORD, to the house of the God of Jacob; and he will teach us of his ways, and we will walk in his paths: for out of Zion shall go forth the law, and the word of the LORD from Jerusalem.

These scriptures show us that in the last days many people will desire to come to the House of God, learn His ways and walk in His paths. When we embrace the Tabernacle Prayer our prayers and worship will go forth out of Zion with power!

In Hebrews 12, we are given a picture of God's dealings with the nation of Israel concerning their priesthood. God is contrasting the Old Covenant with the New Covenant. He begins with Esau, who sold his birthright, and forfeited his call to be a king-priest unto God. This chapter also describes the Israelites rejecting their priesthood when they did not want God to speak to them directly but asked that He speak to them through Moses. But Hebrews 12:22 tells us that we, God's New Testament king-priests, have not rejected our priesthood but have come to Mount Zion the city of the living God, the heavenly Jerusalem!

The Temple Of Solomon – The House of Prayer

God has declared that His House is the Tabernacle or Temple. He also declares it is the House of Prayer! To receive a clear understanding of that statement, let's review Solomon's prayer given at the dedication of the Temple.

I Kin 8:27-30
But will God indeed dwell on the earth? behold, the heaven and heaven of heavens cannot contain thee; how much less this house that I have builded? Yet have thou respect unto the prayer of thy servant, and to his supplication, O LORD my God, to hearken unto the cry and to the prayer, which thy servant prayeth before thee to day: That thine eyes may be open TOWARD this house night and day, even toward the place of which thou hast said, My name shall be there: that thou mayest hearken unto the prayer which thy servant shall make TOWARD this place. And hearken thou to the supplication of thy servant, and of thy people Israel, when they shall pray TOWARD this place: and hear thou in heaven thy dwelling place: and when thou hearest, forgive.

It is very important to understand that the word *"toward"* in the Hebrew means near, with, about, according to, and after.

These scriptures are stating that we are to pray according to the divine order of the House of God!

God's answer to Solomon's prayer below, clearly shows His desire for us to pray in and according to the divine order of God's House! He also promised that His eyes and heart would be there continually.

I Kin 9:3
And the LORD said unto him, I have heard thy prayer and thy supplication, that thou hast made before me: I HAVE HALLOWED THIS HOUSE, which thou hast built, to put my name there for ever; and mine eyes and mine heart shall be there perpetually.

The next scripture is a call to intercession in this holy place, by God Himself.

II Chron 7:14-16
If my people, which are called by my name, shall humble themselves, and pray, and seek my face, and turn from their wicked ways; then will I hear from heaven, and will forgive their sin, and will heal their land. Now mine eyes shall be open, and mine ears ATTENT UNTO THE PRAYER THAT IS MADE IN THIS PLACE. For now have I chosen and SANCTIFIED THIS HOUSE, that my name may be there for ever: and mine eyes and mine heart shall be there perpetually.

In the New Testament, Mark noted that Jesus said all nations shall call His House the House of Prayer. Luke records that Jesus boldly said that HIS HOUSE IS THE HOUSE OF PRAYER!

Luke 19:46
Saying unto them, It is written, MY HOUSE IS THE HOUSE OF PRAYER: but ye have made it a den of thieves.

Let's take a look at what the book of Isaiah says concerning the House of God as the House of Prayer.

Isa 56:7
Even them will I bring to my holy mountain, and make them joyful in MY HOUSE OF PRAYER: their burnt offerings and their sacrifices shall be accepted upon mine altar; FOR MINE HOUSE SHALL BE CALLED AN HOUSE OF PRAYER FOR ALL PEOPLE.

Praise His wonderful name! The Tabernacle is the House of God and the House of prayer for all people!

The Temple of Solomon was a combination of the Tabernacle of Moses and the Tabernacle of David, which is prophetic of the New Testament Church. The Temple combined the divine order and entrance into God's presence with the Davidic order of worship.

The Tabernacle of Moses was a quiet place where the priests solemnly ministered unto the Lord. Only the High Priest, on the Day of Atonement could enter into the presence of God before the Ark. In the Tabernacle of David, he freely ministered in the presence of the Lord, although he was not from the priestly tribe of Levi. He also appointed Levite singers and musicians to worship before the unveiled Ark twenty-four hours a day.

The Temple of Solomon, in its splendor, displayed God's desire for the New Testament Church. God desires His Church to be anointed, wealthy and have the manifestation of the glory of

God. In the past the greatest amount of wealth ever amassed was housed in the Tabernacle and Temples of God, in particular the Temple of Solomon. God desires to release the end-time wealth so we can bring in the end-time harvest of souls.

Solomon's Temple also shows God's desire to have a NATION of kings and priests by the multiplication of the dimensions of the Outer and Inner Courts, and some of the furnishings in the Inner Court. The Tabernacle of Moses had one of each piece of furniture. The Temple of Solomon had one Brazen Altar, one Molten Sea, ten Candlesticks, ten Tables of Shewbread, one Altar of Incense and one Ark of the Covenant.

The Brazen Altar was the same as in the Tabernacle of Moses. The Molten Sea, which sat upon twelve oxen, corresponded to the Brazen Laver. The twelve oxen were symbolic of the apostolic power of the Word of God. The oxen were facing the four corners of the earth, denoting the end-time strength and power of the Word that will cover the earth. There were ten Candlesticks and Tables of Shewbread. Five Candlesticks and Tables were placed on the right side of the Inner Court and the other five were positioned on the left. The number *"five"* signifies the *"grace"* of God that will bring forth the supernatural ability to become His witnesses and intercessors. We will shine forth with the glory of God and have fellowship and communion with Him.

Notice there was only one Brazen Altar, denoting one perfect sacrifice, the Lord Jesus Christ. One place for the priests to wash; signifying that the priesthood could only be cleansed and ready for service by being washed by the water of the Word. Only one Altar of Incense, indicating there is only one way to worship God, in spirit and in truth. Only one Ark of the Covenant, characterizing one God—the Father, Son and Holy Spirit!

In the Tabernacle of Moses the Ark contained three items, which were the Tables of the Law, the Golden Pot of Manna and Aaron's Rod that blossomed. But in the Temple of Solomon the Ark contained only the Tables of the Law. The absence of the Golden Pot of Manna and Aaron's Rod symbolized their prophetic fulfillment in Solomon. He was full of wisdom and knowledge and his kingdom blossomed in fruitfulness. However, the Law was still in the Ark because Jesus, the Word, had not yet come to write His laws upon his heart and in his mind. Solomon had not become a carrier of the indwelling presence of the Lord. But we, the Church, have a new and better covenant!

Heb 8:10-11
For this is the covenant that I will make with the house of Israel after those days, saith the Lord; I will put my laws into their mind, and write them in their hearts: and I will be to them a God, and they shall be to me a people: And they shall not teach every man his neighbour, and every man his brother, saying, Know the Lord: FOR ALL SHALL KNOW ME, FROM THE LEAST TO THE GREATEST.

As we, pray according to the Pattern of Moses' Tabernacle and worship in the Pattern of David's Tabernacle, we will manifest the splendor, glory and wealth of Solomon's Temple! Then all men will see God's awesome power and His manifested glory!

Chapter Nine

Elijah

Mal 4:4-6
Remember ye the law of Moses my servant, which I commanded unto him in Horeb for all Israel, with the statutes and judgments. Behold, I will send you Elijah the prophet before the coming of the great and dreadful day of the LORD: And he shall turn the heart of the fathers to the children, and the heart of the children to their fathers, lest I come and smite the earth with a curse.

Before we begin our study of Elijah, we must lay a foundation that will help our understanding of the prophetic significance of his life. Elijah was a Prophet of God commissioned to revive the Law of Moses and the covenant in the hearts of the Israelites. In other words, Elijah was to bring a revival of *"true worship"* to the Heavenly Father. Our commission as king-priests is the same as that of Elijah. We are to bring a revival of true worship to the Heavenly Father upon this earth!

The Apostolic And Prophetic Anointing

Elijah was an *"apostolic"* Prophet who established the will and order of God in the land. Elijah also moved in an anointing and power that was astounding. It is time for us to take a good look at this power and the message that God has placed inside of the life of Elijah. Let's begin by looking at where we are, as a Church, in regard to the anointing.

Eph 4:11-13
And he gave some, apostles; and some, prophets; and some, evangelists; and some, pastors and teachers; For the perfecting of the saints, for the work of the ministry, for the edifying of the body of Christ: Till we all come in the unity of the faith, and of the knowledge of the Son of God, unto a perfect man, unto the measure of the stature of the fulness of Christ:

For the last 2,000 years the Church has been, in most cases, three-dimensional. We have recognized the ministry of the Evangelist, Pastor and Teacher. Ephesians 4:11-13 describes five ministry gifts that are to equip and bring the Body of Christ to perfection. In these last days God is restoring the ministry of the Apostle and Prophet.

The Apostle has *"breakthrough"* anointing and the ability to establish and bring order. The Prophet has the ability to hear the voice of the Lord and to declare His Word. The apostolic and prophetic anointings are in the process of being restored to the Church to make it complete.

Every believer should have the benefit of these five anointings. This does not mean that he will hold these offices, but each should have the uniqueness of each anointing operating in his life. This can be achieved by praying the Word of God according to Pattern. When we pray according to Pattern, we will find that we have the breakthrough anointing of the Apostle, and we will declare the Word of God as the Prophet. We become a Pastor, Evangelist, and Teacher, exercising the power to evangelize the world from our prayer closet! Elijah was a Prophet but he also had all of these anointings manifested in him. He ministered to Israel as the Apostle, the Prophet, the Pastor, the Teacher and the Evangelist and brought down the glory of God! This is the fullness that God wants to bring to pass in each of us!

Elijah comes on the scene with no recorded genealogy, only an introduction as *"Elijah the Tishbite"*. Elijah's name means *"beloved of Yah"*, and Tishbite means *"converter"*. Yah is God's covenant name. Elijah means to return to the covenant of God. His commission was to turn the children's hearts to their heavenly Father. Malachi 4:4 begins with *"remember ye the law of Moses my servant"*, which means the Tabernacle of God or His prescribed method of approach to Him. Verse 5 states, *"I will send Elijah the Prophet"*, which the Israelites understood to mean that he would come before the Messiah. In other words, God will send Elijah the Prophet to make us remember the Tabernacle of Moses!

Matt 17:10-11
And his disciples asked him, saying, Why then say the scribes that Elias must first come? And Jesus answered and said unto them, ELIAS TRULY SHALL FIRST COME, AND RESTORE ALL THINGS.

The disciples of Jesus asked Him in Matthew 17:10, *"Why then say the scribes that Elias must first come?"* In verse 11, Jesus said that Elijah must come and *"restore all things"*. He goes on to say in verse 12 that John the Baptist was Elijah, meaning he came in the *"spirit and power"* of Elijah to bring repentance and restoration. Just as John the Baptist came to prepare the way of the Lord the first time, the king-priests of God empowered with the apostolic and prophetic anointings are the *"Elijahs"* that will prepare the way for His Second Coming! But notice the order of Malachi 4:4-5, REMEMBERING THE LAW OF MOSES OR THE TABERNACLE WILL PRECEDE THIS REVIVAL! *"The Elijah Anointing"* will make the Church *"remember"* the Law of Moses and usher in the glory of God!

This *"new breed"* of Christian will pick up the prayer mantle of Elijah and go forth in His spirit and power to restore all things by their intercession through the Tabernacle. They will change the hearts of men and produce true worshippers who know their *"Daddy"* God in pure fellowship and intimacy. The true worship will produce a cloud of fragrant perfume that will rise to the Father, and as stated before, the true worship cloud will bring the former and latter rain!

Another powerful key Elijah gave us is reproduction. We are to reproduce ourselves just as Elijah reproduced himself in Elisha. The reproduction of king-priests is beneficial to all because there is no competition. The more king-priests we have, the more power, glory, honor and rain for all of us!

There Will Be No Rain

I Kin 17:1
And Elijah the Tishbite, who was of the inhabitants of Gilead, said unto Ahab, As the LORD God of Israel liveth, before whom I stand, there shall not be dew nor rain these years, but according to my word.

In the Northern kingdom of Israel, Ahab and Jezebel were reigning and had led the people into the worship of baal. They were very evil and Jezebel had the prophets of the Lord murdered. The Lord sent Elijah to tell Ahab of His impending judgment upon the land. The word of the Lord to Ahab was that there would be no rain but according to the word of Elijah. At that time, the worshippers of these idols thought their gods controlled the weather. God chose a drought to show them Who really was in control of the weather! In I Kings 17:2-7, the Lord told Elijah to go to Cherith, which means to *"cut covenant"*. It was here that God supernaturally fed him and took care of all of his needs. Today, our power comes from knowing our covenant to be king-priests unto the Lord, and then He will supernaturally care for us.

The Widow Of Zarephath

I Kin 17:8-9
And the word of the LORD came unto him, saying, Arise, get thee to Zarephath, which belongeth to Zidon, and dwell there: behold, I have commanded a widow woman there to sustain thee.

The Lord directed Elijah to a widow in Zarephath, who would sustain him until He was ready to bring rain upon the earth. As we all know God made supernatural provision for Elijah, the widow, and her son throughout the drought. During this time the widow's son became sick and died, however this incident demonstrates to us the awesome power that Elijah walked in.

I Kin 17:21-22
And he stretched himself upon the child three times, and cried unto the LORD, and said, O LORD my God, I pray thee, let this child's soul come into him again. And the

LORD HEARD THE VOICE OF ELIJAH; and the soul of the child came into him again, and he revived.

Prior to this incident, there was no account of anyone being raised from the dead. But Elijah stretched himself upon the child three times, and prayed for his soul to return to him. The scripture says; *the Lord heard the voice of Elijah"*. God will always hear and respond to the *"voice of the prophetic"*. The prophetic voice on the earth brings life out of death. In verse 24, it is fascinating to note that the woman responds by saying: *"now by this I know that thou art a man of God, and that the word of the Lord in thy mouth is truth"*. The supernatural provision did not totally convince her he was a man of God and that he spoke truth. It was the ability to BRING LIFE, WHERE THERE WAS DEATH!

Praying according to Pattern is actually moving in the spirit of prophecy. Revelation 19:10 states, *"the testimony of Jesus is the spirit of prophecy"*. So it shall be, that those speaking with the prophetic voice of the Lord, testifying of Jesus from the front gate to the Holy of Holies, will be heard and God will bring life where there was death all over the world!

Showdown At Mount Carmel

I Kin 18:1
And it came to pass after many days, that the word of the LORD came to Elijah in the third year, saying, Go, shew thyself unto Ahab; and I will send rain upon the earth.

After 3-1/2 years Elijah is told by the Lord to present himself to Ahab, and He will bring rain upon the earth. In I Kings 18:19-24, Elijah presents himself to Ahab and instructs him to have all the prophets of baal and the children of Israel to gather at

Mount Carmel. He then begins to reason with the Israelites, in an effort to bring them to repentance.

To end all dispute, Elijah called for two bullocks to be sacrificed and then declared the god that answered by fire would be God. Everyone agreed to those terms and the prophets of baal worked in vain to get their god to answer. But a god that does not hear, speak or see cannot answer (I Kings 18:26-29).

The Evening Sacrifice

According to I Kings 18:30-32, Elijah repaired the altar that had been torn down. The *"apostolic-prophetic"* anointing will always repair that which was torn down and bring restoration of that which was lost. In repairing the altar, he used twelve foundation stones symbolic of the twelve sons of Jacob. Elijah was acting as a priest, restoring "true worship" for all of Israel! The sacrifice was prepared and covered three times with four barrels of water (I Kings 18:33-35). Three is always prophetic of the Godhead, the Father, Son, and Holy Spirit and our praise and worship must include them all. Water is symbolic of the Word and we must water our sacrifice of praise with the Word, if we expect God to respond with His fire. In all, there were twelve barrels of water representing the apostolic fullness of the Word that will bring the fire!

The prophets of baal tried from morning until the time of the evening sacrifice. The evening sacrifice in the Temple at Jerusalem was 3:00 p.m. It was at this appointed time Elijah was to offer his sacrifice. He was observing the order in Jerusalem! Then Elijah prayed to the only true God and He answered by fire, the people fell on their faces and began to worship declaring *"the Lord He is God"*.

I Kin 18:37-39
HEAR ME, O LORD, HEAR ME, THAT THIS PEOPLE MAY KNOW THAT THOU ART THE LORD GOD, AND THAT THOU HAST TURNED THEIR HEART BACK AGAIN. *Then the fire of the LORD fell, and consumed the burnt sacrifice, and the wood, and the stones, and the dust, and licked up the water that was in the trench. And when all the people saw it, they fell on their faces: and they said, THE LORD, HE IS THE GOD; THE LORD, HE IS THE GOD.*

Elijah then purged the land by killing the false prophets of Jezebel (I Kings 18:40).

In summary, on Mount Carmel there was repentance, turning back to the Lord in true worship and a redeeming of the land. Mount Carmel, which means a fruitful field, garden and orchard, could now live up to its name. In our season, praying according to Pattern or remembering the Law of Moses will create powerful sacrifices of praise that will manifest the presence of God. It will also destroy demonic forces and redeem the land so that it can bring forth the fruit of the earth.

The Sound Of Abundance Of Rain

I Kin 18:41-45
And Elijah said unto Ahab, Get thee up, eat and drink; for there is a SOUND OF ABUNDANCE OF RAIN. So Ahab went up to eat and to drink. And Elijah went up to the top of Carmel; and he cast himself down upon the earth, and put his face between his knees, And said to his servant, Go up now, look toward the sea. And he went up, and looked, and said, There is nothing. And he said, GO AGAIN SEVEN TIMES. And it came to pass at the SEVENTH TIME, that he said, Behold, there ariseth a LITTLE CLOUD OUT OF THE SEA, LIKE A MAN'S HAND. And he said, Go up, say unto Ahab, Prepare thy chariot, and get thee down, that the rain stop thee not. And it came to pass in the mean while, that the heaven was black with clouds and wind, and

there was a great rain. And Ahab rode, and went to Jezreel.

This drought was caused by the Israelites forsaking the Law of Moses and their covenant. However, it was repentance, cleansing by the blood, and a return to true worship that produced the abundant rain of God's blessings.

Elijah's servant looked seven times before the cloud appeared, while Elijah was praying. This is a prophetic picture of what the Father is doing in His people. We have Elijah whose name means *"beloved of Yah"*. *"Yah"* is our covenant God, so Elijah is a prophetic type of Jesus. He is sending forth the Holy Spirit, His Servant, to look *"seven"* times towards the *"sea"* for the cloud, a sign of rain. The *"sea"* is symbolic of the people of God. Jesus our High Priest is interceding for us and the Holy Spirit is moving upon God's people desperately searching for true worshippers who will produce the true worship cloud so God can bring the rain!

The number *"seven"* always denotes perfection or completeness. The Tabernacle Prayer has seven steps to enter into the Holy of Holies! THE PERFECTION OF PRAYER WAS NEEDED TO PRODUCE THE WORSHIP CLOUD FOR THE RAIN! We cannot produce a "perfect" worship cloud in the Outer or Inner Courts, but only in the Holy of Holies as we worship at the Mercy Seat! The cloud was described as a little cloud like a man's hand, which is the worship cloud coming out of king-priests! Glory to God! It is the perfection of prayer that will produce all, from the fullness of the Saints, to the fullness of the harvest. It is the divine order of prayer that will accomplish all of these things!

Elijah's Journey

I Kin 19:8
And he arose, and did eat and drink, and went in the strength of that meat forty days and forty nights unto Horeb the mount of God.

After this great wave of anointing lifted, Elijah was running from Jezebel because she threatened to kill him. He also asked the Lord to take his life (I Kings 19:1-6). Elijah was a true servant of God, who knew his limitations. Like Elijah, we all should come to the realization that without the presence and power of God we can do nothing. The Lord supernaturally fed him and he journeyed across the wilderness to mount Horeb in the mountains of Sinai where Moses received the Law, statutes and the Tabernacle pattern. God is telling us in so many different ways to return to His divine order!

What Are You Doing Here?

I Kin 19:12-13
...and after the fire a STILL SMALL VOICE. And it was so, when Elijah heard it, that HE WRAPPED HIS FACE IN HIS MANTLE, and went out, and stood in the entering in of the cave. And, behold, there came a voice unto him, and said, WHAT DOEST THOU HERE, ELIJAH?

God asked Elijah *"What doest thou here?"* Elijah was in a cave rehearsing his problem to the Lord. He told God that he had been very zealous for Him, but the Israelites had forsaken His covenant, killed His prophets and he was the only one left and in danger of losing his life (I Kings 19:10).

The Lord told Elijah to stand upon the mountain before Him. According to I Kings 19:11-12, there was a wind, earthquake, and fire and we are told the Lord was not in any of these things. But after the fire there was a *"still small voice"*. Elijah only came out of the cave when he heard the *"still small voice"* of the Holy Spirit. When he came out, he was wrapped in his mantle. This mantle was a prayer shawl called the tallith.

In Hebrew the word *"mantle"* means a garment that signified prayer that is glorious, powerful, and excellent and it also symbolized the Tabernacle of Moses! Moses instructed the children of Israel to make this garment as a reminder of their covenant (Numbers 15:38-39). The Jews would wear it across their shoulders and when they wanted to pray they would place it over their heads and it became a mini-tabernacle in which to pray and worship the Lord. ELIJAH RESPONDED TO THE VOICE OF THE HOLY SPIRIT AND HE CAME OUT WRAPPED IN HIS MINI-TABERNACLE THAT SYMBOLIZED THE GLORY, POWER AND EXCELLENCE OF PRAYER!

Now let's look at the big picture, here we have Elijah in the place where Moses received the Law, the statutes, and the Tabernacle pattern from God. Then we have the Holy Spirit asking him the most powerful question. The Holy Spirit is asking each one of us the same question, which is in reality a wake up call, "WHAT ARE YOU DOING HERE?" When we respond to that wake up call by becoming the king-priests of the Lord, we will manifest His glory!

The Anointing Of Elisha

God tells Elijah to anoint three people to bring about his judgment (I Kings 19:15-18). He said that whoever escaped the sword of Hazael, Jehu would slay. Whoever escaped the sword of Jehu, Elisha would slay. God chose at this point to tell

Elijah that He had reserved 7,000 in Israel that had remained loyal to Him. We see the number *"seven"* again. God had a perfect remnant that would assist in destroying the enemy. Just as it is today, God has a remnant of king-priests who will bring about the destruction of all God's enemies by praying according to Pattern.

Let's take a look at the anointing of Elisha:

I Kin 19:19
So he departed thence, and found Elisha the son of Shaphat, who was plowing with twelve yoke of oxen before him, and he with the twelfth: and Elijah passed by him, and cast his mantle upon him.

The name *"Elisha"* means God of supplication and riches and also strength and might. *"Shaphat"* means to judge or execute judgment. Elisha, the son of Shaphat, represents divine prayer that is rich, full of power, and executes the judgment of God. Notice that Elisha was plowing when Elijah cast his mantle upon him. Plowing is prophetic of sowing the seed of the Word of God. You know God could have chosen to replace Elijah with an established prophet from the school of the prophets, but He chose a *"sower"!* Praise God for his manifold wisdom! It also states that Elisha was with the twelfth yoke of oxen. The number twelve represents duplication and to accumulate. It is also the number of divine government and apostolic fullness! When we pray according to Pattern, we sow the Word of God; execute judgment and duplicate king-priests to bring in the end-time harvest of souls.

At Mount Sinai God asked Elijah, *"What are you doing here?"* Isn't it interesting that after Elijah discovered what his purpose was, the next thing we see him *"doing"* is casting his prayer shawl (mini-tabernacle) upon Elisha and anointing him? It is also important to note Elisha's name represents POWERFUL PRAYER TO DEFEAT THE ENEMIES OF THE LORD! Once we enter our king-priest ministry and duplicate ourselves, we will utterly destroy the enemies of the Lord!

The Pathway Of Elijah

According to II Kings 2:1-6, there were four places that Elijah and Elisha went before Elijah was taken to heaven. These places, Gilgal, Bethel, Jericho and Jordan are prophetic of our calling as king-priests. GILGAL means to commit, remove, roll away, and to trust. We must commit ourselves to our holy calling to pray in divine order and remove all prior traditions so we can obey the Lord.

When we learn to do these things in our relationship with Him, we are ready to go to Bethel. BETHEL means the House of God or Temple. There is no way around it, we must pray according to the divine order God has set in His House. It also means to begin to build, obtain children, repair, and set up. When we pray according to Pattern, we will build the House of God, duplicate ourselves and set up the Kingdom of God upon this earth.

JERICHO is the third stop, and it means to blow, perceive, touch, and make of quick understanding. God will do a quick work in these last days bringing His sons to maturity by the power of the Holy Spirit. This will take place if we create the proper atmosphere by praying the Word of God over them so they will be able to receive.

The last place is JORDAN, which means to bring down (abundantly), put down, subdue, and take down. This is warfare! As previously illustrated, God has provided the safest and most powerful way to do warfare in His House of Prayer. When we perform warfare in this way, which is simply praying in divine order, we will completely subdue and destroy our enemies!

In II Kings 2:9-10, Elisha asked for a double portion of the anointing that was upon Elijah. Elijah said, in essence, if you *"SEE ME GO"*, you will receive your request. When Elisha saw him leave he declared *"my father, my father, the chariot of Israel, and the horsemen thereof"*. The word *"chariot"* means a vehicle, team and army. The word *"Israel"* means those who will rule as God having power with God and man. The *"horsemen"* means a driver of the chariot or army who will separate, wound, scatter, declare and sting. In essence, it means an army that will have the power of God to destroy demonic forces!

Elisha received the PRAYER MANTLE of Elijah and the double-portion anointing to ride upon the High Places and destroy demonic forces in the heavenlies. If we can SEE THE TRUTH of our covenant to be king-priests unto God, we will also receive the mantle of Elijah and a double portion of the apostolic-prophetic anointing. This anointing will turn us into *"Elijahs"* who will ride upon the High Places of the earth destroying the enemies of the Lord, preparing the way for His Second Coming!

The Elijah Anointing

As you can see from this prophetic parallel of Elijah, drought conditions are produced by idolatry and forsaking of the covenant. But when the divine order of the Law of Moses is adhered to, which is true repentance, cleansing by the blood, and true worship, there will be restoration and the rain of God's blessings will be abundant.

Again, we want to emphasize that *"remembering the Law of Moses"*, the *"Elijah Anointing"*, will precede the revival. When we become like Elijah, realizing our covenant and holy calling, we become *"beloved of Yah"*. By this we understand that we are in covenant with God and His provision for us will never fail. We remember His Word and our covenant by declaring them and testifying of the Lord Jesus Christ all the way through the Tabernacle.

The Lord's response will be to hear the voice of the prophetic and bring life out of death, thereby convincing the world that God is in us! As we approach Him according to His divine order, we gain the ability to walk in such close fellowship and intimacy with the Lord that we can freely come and go in and out of His presence. We are transfigured as we ascend into the holy mountain of God according to Pattern. We also have the power to confront demonic forces with the apostolic-prophetic anointing and bring them down in the name of Jesus!

As we stand in the gap and repent for the world, we apply the Blood of Jesus to all in prayer. This type of intercession turns their hearts to the Father bringing them to repentance. As king-priests, praying in divine order, we bring them into true worship unto the Lord. Please understand that Elijah needed the PERFECTION OF PRAYER for the rain to come and so do we! The *"SON"* of God heats the *"living water"* within us, when we pray and worship in perfection. The vapors are then released to form a cloud of worship. The cloud shaped like a man's hand is symbolic of the five-fold anointing coming to perfection in king-priests. This worship cloud will produce an abundance of rain, which is needed for the end-time harvest of souls. The *"Elijah Anointing"* gives us great power to declare and decree the Word of God from the High Places, manifesting His purposes and His glory upon the earth!

Chapter Ten

The Priesthood

I Peter 2:9
But ye are a chosen generation, a royal priesthood, an holy nation, a peculiar people; that ye should shew forth the praises of him who hath called you out of darkness into his marvellous light:

In this scripture we are told that we are a royal priesthood and a holy nation to *"shew"* forth the praises of God. As we learned earlier, our covenant is a covenant to enter into this royal priesthood. Therefore, it is our duty to know and declare the things that God has done, is doing, and will do. The perfect description of the Lord and all He has come to accomplish is found in the Tabernacle. As king-priests, we are to declare and decree the praises of our Lord Jesus Christ according to the Pattern of the Tabernacle.

Another important aspect of our priesthood is the understanding and celebration of the Feasts of the Lord.

Leviticus 23:1-2
And the LORD spake unto Moses, saying, Speak unto the children of Israel, and say unto them, Concerning the Feasts of the LORD, which ye shall proclaim to be holy convocations, even these are my Feasts.

As New Testament priests, we are to understand the Jewish culture and traditions of celebrating these holy days. Why? The word *"Feasts"* in the Hebrew means holy appointments with God! These are the Father's holy appointed times to meet with us and release His blessings. Additionally, the word *"convocations"* mean rehearsals. These Feasts or holy appointed times are prophetic rehearsals of what God has done or will do in the future. After you discover the date of each celebration, ask the Holy Spirit how He wants you to observe or celebrate them. Above all, He would like you to pray over the earth during these special times. We have been totally blessed and in awe during each celebration from the wisdom, love, revelation and prayer that the Holy Spirit brings forth on these special times.

The Israelites celebrated seven major Feasts of the Lord and they are as follows:

Passover - *Mar/Apr* - *(Salvation By The Blood Of Jesus)*
- **Passover** - Celebration of the deliverance of the Israelites from bondage.
- **Unleavened Bread** - Celebration of the separation from the old life.
- **First Fruits** - Consecration of the first fruits of the barley harvest.

Pentecost - *May/Jun* - *(Baptism In The Holy Spirit)*
- **Pentecost** - Celebration marking the completion of the wheat harvest and a memorial to the Israelites receiving the Law, Statutes, and Tabernacle Pattern.

Tabernacles - *Sep/Oct* - *(Fullness Of King-Priest Ministry)*
- **Trumpets** - New Year and time of preparing the people for the Day of Atonement.
- **Day of Atonement** - The day of national repentance and cleansing from sin.
- **Tabernacles** - Celebration of God's supernatural provision in the wilderness and the future hope of entering His rest. It was also a celebration of the final ingathering of the fruit harvest.

As mentioned earlier in this book, the Feasts of the Lord also represent a prophetic timeline for the Church as well as phases in the life of the believer. But it is also interesting to note these Feasts follow the Pattern of the Tabernacle of Moses. The **Feast of Passover** exemplifies the Brazen Altar. This is where we receive total deliverance by the Blood of the Lamb of God. The Brazen Laver represents the **Feast of Unleavened Bread** and **First Fruits.** It is here that we are separated and consecrated unto God by the washing of the water by the Word. The Candlestick, Table of Shewbread and Altar of Incense symbolize the **Feast of Pentecost**. We are anointed and illuminated with the power of the Holy Spirit at the Candlestick. Then we become intercessors and have communion with God at the Table of Shewbread. Subsequently, we enter into worship in spirit and in truth at the Altar of Incense.

The Church has prophetically fulfilled the first two Feast seasons, which are Passover and Pentecost. The next Feast to be fulfilled is Tabernacles. The Feast of Tabernacles is identified with the Holy of Holies and the Ark of the Covenant. The **Feast of Trumpets** will be fulfilled when we understand and declare and decree our covenant. A shofar or ram's horn used as the trumpet for this Feast is symbolic of the Abrahamic Covenant when God supplied the ram for the sacrifice. In essence, to blow the trumpet, means to "DECLARE OUR COVENANT". We will fulfill this prophetic picture by becoming king-priests and declaring our covenant promises. And by praying according to Pattern, we will birth an attitude of repentance and restoration as displayed on the **Day of Atonement**. We will then complete the **Feast of Tabernacles**, with a great harvest of souls, and we will enter into the final rest of God! Glory!!!

The Priestly Garments

Ex 28:21
And the stones shall be with the names of the children of Israel, twelve, according to their names, like the engravings of a signet; every one with his name shall they be according to the twelve tribes.

According to Exodus 28:21, the breastplate of the High Priest contained twelve stones that represented the tribes of Israel.

There were also two stones on the shoulders of the ephod that were inscribed with the names of the twelve tribes (Exodus 28:9-12). As New Testament king-priests, we bear the same stones. These stones now represent the unsaved, world leadership, the Body of Christ, and the nation of Israel. Isn't it startling that we have been given the responsibility to pray for physical and spiritual Israel, yet most of us have never been taught to do this? Most intercessors have been taught to focus on a particular situation or group of people, most likely, immediate surroundings. Our priesthood requires that we pray for ALL men. We can target certain people or situations ONLY AFTER we have fulfilled our priestly duty.

I Tim 2:1-2
I exhort therefore, that, first of all, supplications, prayers, intercessions, and giving of thanks, be made for ALL MEN; For kings, and for all that are in authority; that we may lead a quiet and peaceable life in all godliness and honesty.

As you can see in I Timothy 2:1, we are to pray for the unsaved, world leadership, the Body of Christ, and Israel which encompasses *"all men"*. The call to pray for the nation of Israel has been largely unfulfilled by the Church. Psalms 122:6 states, *"Pray for the peace of Jerusalem: they shall prosper that love thee"*. This call is vitally important to the purposes of God. There cannot be a true and lasting peace in Jerusalem until the return of the Lord Jesus Christ! Our Messiah was born in Israel and at His Second Coming will return to Israel. Therefore, when we pray for the peace of Jerusalem, we are praying for the completion of all God's purposes for mankind! Furthermore, we have been adopted into this Jewish family therefore we have an obligation to pray for our family. There is also a blessing given to those who pray for Israel. We, the

Church, are to continually pray for the peace of Jerusalem, bless them and seek their highest good.

Another important aspect of the priestly garment was the robe. The hem of it was encircled with bells and pomegranates.

Ex 28:34-35
A golden bell and a pomegranate, a golden bell and a pomegranate, upon the hem of the robe round about. And it shall be upon Aaron to minister: and his sound shall be heard when he goeth in unto the holy place before the LORD, and when he cometh out, that he die not.

The golden bells were symbolic of the gifts of the Spirit (I Corinthians 12:8-10). The pomegranates were symbolic of the fruit of the spirit (Galatians 5:22-23). As Christians, we are out of balance when we do not have the fruit and the gifts operating in perfect balance. Without the love, character, and power of God we cannot be true witnesses. It is possible to operate in the gifts without development of the fruit in our lives. Additionally, it is possible to have well-developed fruit, without the gifts. When we have this balance, as we minister before the Lord, we will produce life and not death. Our Lord will judge us according to how well we have achieved this balance.

Ex 28:36-38
And thou shalt make a plate of pure gold, and grave upon it, like the engravings of a signet, HOLINESS TO THE LORD. And thou shalt put it on a blue lace, that it may be upon the mitre; upon the forefront of the mitre it shall be. And it shall be upon Aaron's forehead, that Aaron may bear the iniquity of the holy things, which the children of Israel shall hallow in all their holy gifts; and it shall be always upon his forehead, that they may be accepted before the LORD.

The mitre of the High Priest with the engraving, *"HOLINESS UNTO THE LORD"*, signified righteousness. God looked at the High Priest as the head over Israel. Through the holiness that was imputed to the High Priest, all of Israel was sanctified. This is the type and shadow of the Lord Jesus Christ, our High Priest, Who sanctified us through His holiness. We, as king-priests of the Lord, have been graced to share the holiness of the Lord and can sanctify others in prayer.

The Vision Of Jesus As High Priest

I Peter 2:5
Ye also, as lively stones, are built up a spiritual house, an holy priesthood, to offer up spiritual sacrifices, acceptable to God by Jesus Christ.

One evening in Church, in the midst of praise and worship, I had a vision of the Lord Jesus Christ dressed in His priestly garments. Very prominent in this vision, were the twelve stones in His breastplate. At first I did not understand what He was trying to show me. In order to emphasize His purpose, He pulled me close to Him and pressed my face into the breastplate. When I stepped back, I looked directly into His breastplate. In each stone, I beheld distant lands. Then I saw people of every nation reaching out of His breastplate. I began to make the connection of the importance of our priestly function concerning prayer for all nations.

Suddenly the faces began to change. At first, their faces reflected joy, but now I could see terror in their faces and a brood of demonic forces over them. Then I looked directly into the Lord's eyes and saw an incredible sadness. He was asking me to continue to pray for the people, which are His precious stones. There was such sadness in His heart, because most have not realized their responsibility to become king-priests and pray for all men!

One of the definite benefits of praying for people as precious stones is that we do not see them in their circumstances as sick, bound, or lost. But we behold them as precious stones, unique and beautiful, which is the way God sees them. Praying in this manner is not grievous and most importantly, does not overload the intercessor with negative aspects of their circumstances. Their condition may be a fact, but it is not the truth. The truth is, by His stripes we are healed! We pray the *"truth"* of the Word of God over them, changing their facts with God's truth.

Repentance And The Gate

The word *"repent"* essentially means to be sorry and have a change of heart in turning back to God. When *"re-pent"* is broken down, *"re"* means back, again, anew and *"pent"* means up. This is where we get the word penthouse, denoting the highest level of a building. Therefore, when we repent, we return to the highest level with God. Repentance is vitally important to prayer. It is important because God's Word states in Psalms 66:18, if we regard iniquity in our hearts, the LORD WILL NOT HEAR US. According to I John 1:9, if we confess our sins, He is faithful and just to forgive us and to cleanse us from ALL UNRIGHTEOUSNESS.

David's Repentance

Ps 51:4
Against thee, thee only, have I sinned, and done this evil in thy sight: that thou mightest be justified when thou speakest, and be clear when thou judgest.

David was guilty of adultery with Bathsheba and the murder of her husband, Uriah. According to the Law, he should have been sentenced to death. Both sins carried a penalty of death. However, David asked God for deliverance from *"bloodguiltiness"* and his repentance reversed the death sentence. David, having a revelation of God's love and mercy, appealed to Him on that basis and his life was spared. In Psalms 51:4, David declares that his sin was against God alone. This is a very powerful element of repentance. When we do anything to harm others or ourselves we are in fact sinning against God. Therefore true repentance involves the acknowledgment that we sinned not only against our fellowman but also against God.

God couldn't help but be touched by David's plea for deliverance and cleansing! David also asked not be cast out of God's presence and that the Holy Spirit not be taken from him. He then asked for restoration of the joy of his salvation and promises to convert sinners to God. David first thought of offering sacrifices for his sins. In Psalms 51:16, he says he knows God does not desire burnt offerings without true heart repentance. In verse 17, he states a broken spirit and a broken and contrite heart are what God desires. David goes on to say when he brings these heart attitudes to God, then his burnt offerings will be acceptable unto Him.

We can imagine how pleased God must have been with this repentance! God will be pleased with us also when we repent with a broken and contrite heart. Too often, our repentance is shallow and therefore our sacrifice of praise and worship to the Lord is unacceptable. We must understand, as David did, God desires us to repent so we can be pure and holy, so our sacrifice of praise will be pleasing unto Him.

In the Old Testament the priests were instructed to wash before performing any priestly duties, this was their repentance. If they did not heed this instruction, it would result in their death. Today we do not die physically, but our prayers do suffer a form of spiritual death – they are not as effective.

Ex 30:20-21
When they go into the tabernacle of the congregation, they shall wash with water, that they die not; or when they come near to the altar to minister, to burn offering made by fire unto the LORD: So they shall wash their hands and their feet, that they die not: and it shall be a statute for ever to them, even to him and to his seed throughout their generations.

As New Testament king-priests, we are responsible to pray for ourselves and intercede for the precious and lively stones of God. So it is important we wash ourselves with the water of the Word in repentance, before we begin to minister unto the Lord. We serve a holy God, and His holiness does not allow sin in His presence. This important step prepares us to minister unto the Lord.

The Gate – Hallowed Be Thy Name

As we enter His gates with thanksgiving, we hallow the name of the Lord. First of all we acknowledge He is our Father and we offer thanksgiving on that basis. We thank Jesus for revealing the Father-heart of God to us. We thank our Father for His grace and goodness in bringing us into perfect relationship with Him.

We then begin to hallow the names of the Lord. To hallow means to make holy, sanctify and consecrate. The Lord's name, of course, is already holy and above every name in the universe. However, we need to acknowledge His holiness and majesty by exalting the names by which He has revealed Himself. This is our basis for thanksgiving, praise and worship. It would be beneficial to obtain a book listing the redemptive names of God. In the redemptive names of Yahweh or Jehovah, He has revealed aspects of our covenant inheritance. God will respond to us and manifest our blessings based upon our revelation knowledge of His nature and character. So when we hallow or consecrate His name, He will become everything we need Him to be!

The Blood Has A Voice

Gen 4:10
And he said, What hast thou done? the voice of thy brother's blood crieth unto me from the ground.

Heb 12:24
And to Jesus the mediator of the new covenant, and to the blood of the sprinkling, that speaketh better things than that of Abel.

A friend of ours shattered our theology one day when she said; we do not understand what was happening in the Garden of

Gethsemane. She went on to say that Jesus was not shrinking from the thoughts of His impending death. She declared that in the Garden of Gethsemane, Jesus was actually trying to pass the Blood from His body! We were so shocked, yet we found ourselves meditating upon that thought.

Matt 26:38-39
Then saith he unto them, My soul is exceeding sorrowful, even unto death: tarry ye here, and watch with me. And he went a little farther, and fell on his face, and prayed, saying, O my Father, if it be possible, LET THIS CUP PASS FROM ME: nevertheless not as I will, but as thou wilt.

At the Last Supper Jesus clearly states that this cup is for the remission of sins!

Matt 26:26-28
And as they were eating, Jesus took bread, and blessed it, and break it, and gave it to the disciples, and said, Take, eat; this is my body. And he took THE CUP, and gave thanks, and gave it to them, saying, Drink ye all of it; For this is my blood of the new testament which is shed for many for the remission of sins.

During the Passover meal, four cups of wine were consumed. The first cup was called the **"Cup of Sanctification"** because it consecrated the whole meal. The second cup was called the **"Cup of Praise"**. The third cup was called the **"Cup of Blessing"** or **"Cup of Redemption"** which represented the blood of the Passover Lamb. The fourth cup was called the **"Cup of Elijah"**. It was the third cup Jesus was speaking of in Matthew 26:27-28 when He declared this cup called the **"Cup of Blessing"**, was His Blood that was shed for our sins. In I Corinthians 10:16 the Apostle Paul confirmed that the Blood of Jesus is the **"Cup of Blessing"**.

I Cor 10:16
The CUP OF BLESSING which we bless, is it not the communion of the blood of Christ? The bread which we break, is it not the communion of the body of Christ?

We began to question why Jesus, the Lamb slain before the foundation of the world, born for the purpose of dying, would seemingly not want to die! Why would He rebuke Peter so strongly for trying to prevent His death, and then pray to escape it Himself?

We have been taught Jesus was sorrowful regarding the separation from God the Father that He knew He would experience when He allowed Himself to be made sin for us. While this is true, we have misunderstood what Jesus was really trying to accomplish in the Garden of Gethsemane. He was trying to pass the Blood, which was the **"cup of blessing"**, from His body to redeem mankind! When Jesus prayed that the cup pass FROM Him, He was actually asking for this cup to pass OUT of Him and not AWAY from Him. The Greek word **"pass"** means basically **"out of"** and not **"away from"**.

Isa 53:10-11
Yet it pleased the LORD to BRUISE him; he hath put him to grief: when thou shalt make his soul an offering for sin, he shall see his seed, he shall prolong his days, and the pleasure of the LORD shall prosper in his hand. HE SHALL SEE OF THE TRAVAIL OF HIS SOUL, AND SHALL BE SATISFIED: by his knowledge shall my righteous servant justify many; for he shall bear their iniquities.

We know Jesus knew all things concerning His days upon the earth. He also knew the exact timing of these things. While in the Garden of Gethsemane, Jesus knew Judas had betrayed Him and the Jewish leaders would have him arrested shortly. Knowing His time was limited, Jesus prayed for this cup to pass OUT of Him. The only way that this could be accomplished was for the Father to **BRUISE** Him. The word *"bruise"* means to crush, break, and cause injury without breaking the skin. Ruptured blood vessels and discoloration often characterize this. Bruise also means to hurt, especially psychologically. This bruising caused internal bleeding, therefore causing great drops of Blood to pass from His body.

We have heard doctors say, when a person bleeds from their pores, they are close to death. Can you imagine the delicate balance that had to be achieved, so He could remain alive and still endure the crucifixion? *God the Father had to place the iniquity of all mankind, past, present, and future, upon the sinless Lamb of God. Jesus was not reluctant but more than ready to complete all that was written about Him!* In Matthew 26:38, Jesus asked the disciples to pray with Him. It was during this time that He was waiting on the hand of the Father to bruise Him.

Luke 22:43-44
And there appeared an angel unto him from heaven, STRENGTHENING HIM. And being in an agony he prayed more earnestly: and his sweat was as it were GREAT DROPS OF BLOOD FALLING DOWN TO THE GROUND.

We find in verse 43, an angel strengthened Jesus prior to His sweating great drops of Blood. Please note He was strengthened first; THEN He released the Blood! The angels were sent to strengthen Him so that He could release His Blood, the *"cup of blessing"!*

Have you wondered why the disciples went to sleep? Their spirits could not handle what was taking place. They fell asleep because the atmosphere was filled with all the iniquities of mankind as they were being poured into the sinless soul of Jesus.

In the Garden of Gethsemane Jesus was yielding Himself to the hand of the Father to bruise Him with our iniquities so He could accomplish the TRAVAIL OF HIS SOUL. According to Isaiah 53:11, the Father would see the fruit of this travail and be satisfied.

The Blood Declares The End From The Beginning

Isa 46:9-10
Remember the former things of old: for I am God, and there is none else; I am God, and there is none like me, DECLARING THE END FROM THE BEGINNING, AND FROM ANCIENT TIMES THE THINGS THAT ARE NOT YET DONE, saying, My counsel shall stand, and I will do all my pleasure:

A characteristic of God is that He never does anything without first speaking it or laying a foundation. Gethsemane had to happen before Calvary. The redemption was accomplished in the spirit realm first, then in the physical. The Blood shed for our redemption in Gethsemane was declaring something that was NOT YET DONE!

What happened in the Garden of Gethsemane laid the foundation for the Blood of God to cry out from the earth, then the cross of Calvary fulfilled that cry!

If Gethsemane had not happened, they could not have killed Jesus. Have you noticed there were times that people tried to kill Jesus and He just passed through them? They could not kill Him before this time because there was no death in Him; He was sinless. When He bore our iniquities in the Garden of Gethsemane, He received our penalty of death and our death sentence. Only then was it possible for Jesus to be killed!

The Blood Breaks The Curse

When God judged the sin of Adam, He pronounced a curse upon the ground (Genesis 3:17). In order for Jesus to redeem mankind, He had to start with the dust of the earth, the essence of which man was made. According to Genesis 4:10 and Hebrews 12:24, there is a special property about blood that enables it to speak. Because the Blood of Jesus speaks better things than that of Abel, the Blood Jesus released in Gethsemane was speaking forth and prophesying the redemption of all mankind. The Blood of the last Adam cried for mercy, love, restoration, and reconciliation. The Lord Jesus Christ was redeeming in the Garden of Gethsemane what the first Adam lost in the Garden of Eden. The first Adam lost the glory of God, fellowship, and the ability to be fruitful—to shine with the glory and power of God. Jesus came to break the curse that was upon us so all these things could be restored.

The first reference to the blood speaking or having a voice can be found in Genesis 4:10. God was speaking to Cain about the murder of his brother Abel; *"And he said, What hast thou done? The voice of thy brother's blood crieth unto me from the ground".* Verse 11 states, that now Cain was cursed FROM the earth, which had received his brother's blood at his hand. The innocent blood of Abel spoke and cursed his brother from the earth. Throughout history there has been much innocent blood shed. Can you imagine the curse this blood has been speaking against mankind? The Blood of Jesus that spoke from the earth in Gethsemane broke the curse the earth was speaking against guilty mankind.

Genesis 4:12 states, *"when thou tillest the ground, it shall not henceforth yield unto thee her strength; a fugitive and a vagabond shalt thou be in the earth"*. The curse "FROM" the earth against Cain, was the voice of innocent blood, producing a VAGABOND spirit. The word *"vagabond"* means drifting, aimless, wandering, unsettled, unfixed, purposeless, futile, and pointless.

There is indication in scripture that Abel offered the required blood sacrifice unto the Lord and Cain brought fruits and vegetables, his effort of the flesh (Genesis 4:3-5). He did not bring the blood, which is the ONLY foundation for worship! Instead he became jealous and killed Abel because his blood offering was acceptable worship unto the Lord. Cain's life became a LIVING DEATH, with no aim, no purpose, and no clue because he did not understand the value of the blood! Doesn't that describe a major portion of humanity?

If we do not have a revelation of the power or the importance of the Blood of Jesus, we cannot bring acceptable sacrifices of praise. Therefore, we do not have the life of God and His power in our prayers! Our lives will not line up with the true plan and purpose of God, and cannot yield the maximum harvest. The Blood of Jesus broke that vagabond curse over us, so we could know our TRUE DESTINY and PURPOSE and find REST in Him!

In Leviticus 17:11, we are told that the life of the flesh is in the blood, and God has given it to us upon the altar to make atonement for our souls. It is only the *"Life of God"* that is in the Blood of Jesus that can produce life **out** of death and break the curse of sin and death. The Blood **of** Jesus is the only substance in the universe that could restore everything in every realm, and answer every charge that sin could possibly bring against mankind. The Blood of Jesus is **awesome!**

According to Leviticus 16:14, on the **Day** of Atonement, the blood of the sacrifice was applied to the **Mercy** Seat and seven times before it on the ground. The blood applied seven times on the ground was prophetic of the Blood of Jesus possessing the sum total of perfection to completely **redeem** the earth and we who were made from the earth! It **was** foreshadowing what our Lord accomplished in Gethsemane **when** He sweat great drops of Blood. The Incarnation enabled Jesus to bring the Blood of God to the earth. He carried it for thirty years and released it at the appointed time! Hallelujah, Praise His Wonderful Matchless Name!

When we reflect upon the agonies that **our** Lord went through in the Garden of Gethsemane, it evokes the highest praise from within us. Each day in the Tabernacle Prayer, we extol our conquering hero at the Brazen Altar, which is symbolic of Gethsemane and Calvary. As king-priests, filled with revelation knowledge, we have the power to activate the awesome benefits of the Blood of Jesus. We declare that His Blood has a voice, and this voice speaks redemption, restoration and deliverance!

The Eternal Word

Heb 4:12
For the word of God is quick, and powerful, and sharper than any twoedged sword, piercing even to the dividing asunder of soul and spirit, and of the joints and marrow, and is a discerner of the thoughts and intents of the heart.

The Word of God is the most powerful living force in the universe. According to Psalms 138:2, God exalts His Word above His name. Adam was led by his spirit before he fell into sin. When he decided to follow his emotions instead of the Word of God, his soul and spirit became intermingled. He was no longer spirit-led as God had designed him. He became a being, led by His five senses. The SOUL is the emotions, will, thoughts, and intellect and the SPIRIT is the part of our being that communicates with God. The only force that can divide the soul from the spirit is the living Word of God. Division is necessary so we can walk in the wisdom of God. As king-priests unto God, we are to declare and decree His Word, not our opinions or circumstances, because His Word is all-powerful.

The Cleansing Power Of The Blood And Water

John 19:34
But one of the soldiers with a spear pierced his side, and forthwith came there out blood and water.

Just as God took one of Adams ribs from his side in order to create his wife, the Blood and water came forth out of the side of Jesus to give birth to His bride, the Church. The Blood purchased our redemption, while the water of His Word cleanses us, in order to become His bride. The Blood and the water are two cleansing agents given by the Lord Jesus to redeem us from spiritual death. We are cleansed by applying the Blood of Jesus in prayer, declaring His Word over ourselves and others. This cleansing gives us the ability to draw near unto the Lord (Hebrews 10:22).

The Three That Agree On Earth

I John 5:7-8
For there are three that bear record in heaven, the Father, the Word, and the Holy Ghost: and these three are one. And there are three that bear witness in earth, the spirit, and the water, and the blood: and these three agree in one.

Every piece of the Tabernacle furniture was anointed with the blood of the sacrifice and the anointing oil, which represented the Holy Spirit. Yet we see something significant in the fact the Laver, which was filled with water, was the only one that had the three elements of the power of God. These three elements were the Spirit, the water, and the Blood. So when we speak the Word of God, we employ the three powers of God to establish His Word in the earth. According to Psalms 119:89, the Word is forever settled in heaven. As vessels, cleansed by the Blood, anointed with the Holy Ghost, and washed by the water of the Word, we are to declare God's Word to establish it upon the earth. The result will be that the three that bear record in heaven, the Father, the Word, and the Holy Ghost will back up every word!

Who Do You Say I Am?

Matt 16:15-16
He saith unto them, But whom say ye that I am? And Simon Peter answered and said, THOU ART THE CHRIST, THE SON OF THE LIVING GOD.

The Tabernacle is also called the *"Tabernacle of Testimony"*, which testifies of the Lord Jesus Christ. The Word tells us in Revelation 12:11, that we overcome the devil by the Blood of the Lamb, and by the word of our testimony. The word *"testimony"* comes from a root word that means, *"martyr"*. In essence, that scripture is saying we overcome the devil by the Blood of the Lamb and by our testimony of the life, death, resurrection and total dominion of Jesus Christ! As we testify of Jesus from the front gate all the way into the Holy of Holies through the Tabernacle Prayer, we are destroying the enemy.

Psalms 8:2 states that God has ordained praise to stop the enemy and the avenger. Our praise of Jesus Christ is much more powerful than we had previously imagined. Now we can see why Jesus became so excited when Peter answered His question; *"whom say ye that I am?"* Peter answered, *"Thou art the Christ, the Son of the living God"*. In response to his answer, Jesus blessed him. In Matthew 16:18, Jesus said that upon this revelation, THE DECLARATION OF WHO HE IS, He would build a victorious Church that the gates of Hell would not prevail against! As New Testament king-priests, we are to declare Who Jesus is, all the way through the Tabernacle!

Your Sons And Daughters Shall Prophesy

Joel 2:28-29
And it shall come to pass afterward, that I will pour out my spirit upon all flesh; and your sons and your daughters shall prophesy, your old men shall dream dreams, your young men shall see visions: And also upon the servants and upon the handmaids in those days will I pour out my spirit.

We believe that the king-priests of the Lord, praying the Tabernacle Prayer Pattern, is a fulfillment of Joel 2:28-29. The Book of Joel states, that in the last days God will pour out His Spirit upon all flesh and our sons and daughters shall prophesy. This passage is not describing the five-fold ministry office of the Prophet (Ephesians 4:11-12), or the gift of prophecy as described in I Corinthians 12:10. But what Joel is really saying, is that God's children will prophesy or SPEAK THE WORD! According to Revelation 19:10, the testimony of Jesus *"IS"* the spirit of prophecy! The testimony of Jesus, all the way through the Tabernacle, is the true spirit of prophecy. Praise God, WE ALL CAN AND WILL PROPHESY!

The Light Of The World

John 8:12
Then spake Jesus again unto them, saying, I am the light of the world: he that followeth me shall not walk in darkness, but shall have the light of life.

The *"light of life"* is the glory of God, that we are destined to walk in. In Matthew 5:14, Jesus said we are the light of the world, and a city set upon a hill that cannot be hidden. There have been many prophetic words concerning believers, in these last days, walking in the glory and the power of God. Yet, false humility and unbelief have kept us from declaring it and praying for it to be manifested in our lives.

Rev 1:20
The mystery of the seven stars which thou sawest in my right hand, and the seven golden candlesticks. The seven stars are the angels of the seven churches: and the seven candlesticks which thou sawest are the seven churches.

Revelation 1:20, reveals that the Church of God is represented as seven golden candlesticks. In the Old Testament, the priest would enter into the Holy Place daily to dress the Candlestick. He would first trim the wicks, deposit fresh olive oil, and re-ignite it so it would burn brightly each day.

In prayer, we declare that we are the *"light of the world"*, the golden candlesticks. We then ask the Lord Jesus Christ, our High Priest, to trim our wicks and cut away all things that are not pleasing to Him. We also ask for a fresh refilling of anointing oil and to be set on fire anew. This is the prayer that we pray over the five-fold ministry, the entire Body of Christ, and ourselves.

When there is no hindrance to the *"light"* of God flowing through us, the world will see our good works and glorify our Father in heaven. One of the greatest benefits of having the glory of God manifested upon us is holy protection. God says in Isaiah 4:5, that there will be a *"DEFENSE"* upon the glory. As darkness quickly approaches, every Christian should be clothed in the glory and protection of God.

Intercession And Communion

Intercession

True intercession is praying according to Pattern. The Tabernacle Prayer takes us through repentance. The Blood of Jesus and the water of His Word in the Outer Court cleanse us. As we go beyond the gate of TRUTH, we are illuminated and anointed at the Lampstand. We then prepare for warfare intercession at The Table of Shewbread. However, before warring for anyone---REPENT FOR THEM FIRST! We can use the examples that are in Daniel 9 and Ezra 9. These intercessors identified with and repented for the sins of their nation. Due to the fact that we are free agents, God will not force Himself upon us to love and accept Him. But when we, as king-priests stand in the gap and repent for others, God is faithful to go forth and begin to work in their lives. That is why God is always looking for a man to stand in the gap so judgment can be averted (Ezekiel 22:30).

The next step we must do BEFORE warring is to put on the whole armor of God (Ephesians 6:10-20). Most people begin warfare without this process and they enter the spiritual battlefield unprotected. Entering the battlefield without our armor is spiritual suicide! We have noticed while ministering deliverance, there are people who have spiritual warfare wounds, due to going into battle against the enemy without the proper protection.

It is vitally important to our welfare to put on our armor before entering spiritual warfare. The fiery darts of the wicked one are not felt physically. They wound our spirit man thereby draining us of power and energy. Then slowly but surely it manifests in our soul man bringing about discouragement, hopelessness and other ungodly attitudes. This in turn leaves us open to attacks in our physical bodies. So please understand that we must put on our armor before we get on the battlefield.

Communion

The *"Bread"* represents the broken body of Jesus Christ, which is our nourishment and strength to do battle, to prevail, and overcome. The *"Wine"* represents the shed Blood of Jesus for the remission of our sins. The *"Bread and Wine"* contains the **"Life of God"** needed to defeat every form of darkness in our lives. This life that we are talking about is not life as in a *"breathing entity"*, but it is "zoe"; God's kind of life—victorious life! At the Table of Shewbread, we spiritually partake of communion for all men and receive this *"zoe"* life within us. Another powerful point to recognize is the fact that Jesus came as a man anointed by the Holy Spirit. He defeated all demonic forces as the Son of Man, not as the Son of God. The Holy Spirit also anoints us, and by receiving communion we gain that same power to overcome our enemies.

John 6:53, 56
Then Jesus said unto them, Verily, verily, I say unto you, Except ye eat the flesh of the Son of man, and drink his blood, ye have no life in you. He that eateth my flesh, and drinketh my blood, dwelleth in me, and I in him.

We take communion so God will dwell in us and we will dwell in Him. When we do this, the *"Light and Life of God"* destroys all darkness in and around us and gives us the power and authority to annihilate our enemies.

I Cor 11:26
For as often as ye eat this bread, and drink this cup, ye do show the Lord's death till he come.

This scripture states that we are to declare and decree the Lord's death, resurrection, and glorification every time we receive communion. He said as often as we do this, (take communion), we are to declare His praises! Declaring the victory of the Son of Man and partaking of His flesh and Blood empowers us to become like Him—anointed to destroy the works of the enemy! Each day when we pray according to Pattern, we spiritually partake of communion at the Table of Shewbread and receive His power! At the end of the Prayer, we usually physically take communion.

True Worship

We were created for God's pleasure to bring worship unto Him. We were designed with a *"call to worship"* inside of us. If we do not fulfill that call by worshipping God, we will worship other things. Scenes in the book of Revelation depict continuous worship of the Lord in heaven. Therefore, we can conclude that our worship unto God is a *"timeless"* ministry. In the context of the Tabernacle of Moses, the Altar of Incense was the last piece of furniture encountered before the High Priest could enter into the presence of God. Following the divine pathway from the front gate to the *"place of worship"* is necessary to enter into God's presence.

The Holy Anointing Oil

Ex 30:22-25
Moreover the LORD spake unto Moses, saying, Take thou also unto thee principal spices, of pure MYRRH five hundred shekels, and of sweet CINNAMON half so much, even two hundred and fifty shekels, and of sweet CALAMUS two hundred and fifty shekels, And of CASSIA five hundred shekels, after the shekel of the sanctuary, and of OIL OLIVE an hin: And thou shalt make it an oil of holy ointment, an ointment compound after the art of the apothecary: it shall be an holy anointing oil.

The Tabernacle, furnishings, and the priests were anointed and consecrated with the holy anointing oil (Exodus 32:26-30). This anointing oil was not to be placed upon the flesh of common man, neither could it be reproduced for use anywhere other than the Tabernacle (Exodus 32:32). This oil is symbolic of the Holy Spirit and consisted of five ingredients; which were myrrh, cinnamon, calamus, cassia, and olive oil. These five spices have a prophetic significance concerning worship.

Since five is the number of grace and divine ability, each of the five spices represents a *"grace"* of the Holy Spirit to transform us into true worshippers. The MYRRH represents distillation, which means the process of heating a mixture and condensing the vapor to produce a more pure substance. The fire of the Holy Spirit causes this vaporizing process to purify us and make our prayers ascend on high. It also denotes bitterness, which means dying to self by killing the flesh. CINNAMON means to erect upright rolls and to emit a smell. In other words the power of the Holy Spirit will come upon us, building us up to emit a fragrance pleasing unto the Lord. CALAMUS means to strengthen, recover and possess. The Holy Spirit strengthens our inner man to recover and possess our covenant blessings. CASSIA means to shrivel up, bend the body, and bow down the head or stoop. When we humble ourselves and pray according to Pattern, the Spirit of the Lord increases, and our flesh is diminished. The OLIVE OIL means illuminating oil, to be cheerful and bright. The Holy Spirit is the illuminating oil to bring revelation knowledge and the glory of God upon us.

In summary, the Holy Spirit purifies our prayers, causing us to emit a sweet fragrance unto the Father. We are also strengthened to possess our covenant blessings through humility and revelation knowledge for His glory!

The Holy Worship Incense

Ex 30:34-36
And the LORD said unto Moses, Take unto thee sweet spices, STACTE, and ONYCHA, and GALBANUM; these sweet spices with pure FRANKINCENSE: of each shall there be a like weight: And thou shalt make it a perfume, a confection after the art of the apothecary, tempered together, pure and holy: And thou shalt beat some of it very small, and put of it before the testimony in the tabernacle of the congregation, where I will meet with thee: it shall be unto you most holy.

At the Altar of Incense the priests would burn a specially compounded mixture of spices called the holy incense. This incense produced a cloud of sweet smelling aroma that pleased God and protected the lives of the priests. Every time they ministered in the Holy Place they had to take a handful of incense and place it upon the Altar (Exodus 30:6-8). The five ingredients in the incense were Stacte, Onycha, Galbanum, Frankincense and Salt. STACTE is an aromatic gum that distills gradually by oozing, and it also means to speak by inspiration and to prophesy. In order to exhibit this heart motivation in worship, we must be spontaneous and free flowing. We must also prophesy or speak the Word of the Lord over others and ourselves. ONYCHA is an aromatic mussel (deep-sea shellfish). It also means to peel off by concussion of sound and to roar as a lion. This aspect takes place when we declare and decree the Word of God according to Pattern. We peel off the flesh and become a sweet smelling aroma unto the Lord. GALBANUM is an odorous gum from a gum rosin tree. It also means to be fat, the richest or choice part, the best, and the finest. It simply means that we are to bring the highest and greatest worship to God. FRANKINCENSE is a vegetable resin obtained from a tree and derives its name from a root word to be made *"white"*. When we bring the Frankincense, which represents Jesus, we produce purity in worship. SALT was added to temper the spices. Salt is a purifier, preservative, seasoning and symbolic of our covenant. The salt is also necessary because we can only bring true worship unto God by being in covenant relationship with Him.

Hot coals, that were used to burn the sacrifice at the Brazen Altar, were placed on this Altar to burn the incense. We cannot produce worship without the *"hot coals"* of a committed life toward the Lord, our precious Sacrifice. All of the spices contained in the incense were beaten into a fine powder. The priests had to take a handful of powder and place it on the Altar without dropping one speck. If any fell to the ground the priest would die. As intercessors spiritual death can occur, if any part of our worship is lost or falls to the ground. If spiritual death occurs, our prayers are ineffective and we will not enter into God's presence. Praying according to Pattern not only prepares us, but also teaches us how to please God. We please the Lord when we bring worship qualities of spontaneity, depth, transparency, honesty, and purity with covenant speech (the Word of God).

The Secret Place

Ps 91:1
He that dwelleth in the secret place of the most High shall abide under the shadow of the Almighty.

There was a veil that separated the Inner Court from the Most Holy Place. It was made of fine linen with figures of cherubim woven into it (Exodus 26:31). This veil represented the fullness of the Godhead. When we go beyond the veil, we enter the realm where we can experience the fullness and glory of God. The Holy of Holies was where the presence (Shekinah) of the Lord dwelt. His presence dwelt just above the Mercy Seat, the cover to the Ark of the Covenant, where the blood of the sacrifice was applied. When we reach this point, we are in the Secret Place of the Most High and it is time to worship the Lamb of God at the Mercy Seat! This next section will show us how to worship the Lamb of God to perfection!

The Mercy Of God

On the Day of Atonement the blood of the sacrifice was applied to the Mercy Seat and seven times before it, on the ground (Leviticus 16:14). After the resurrection of Jesus, He entered the heavenly sanctuary with His Blood and placed it on heaven's Mercy Seat. Hebrews 12:24 states the Blood of Jesus speaks better things than that of Abel, but we are not told what these things are.

One day in prayer I asked God what is the Blood of Jesus speaking? God replied by asking me the question; *"Where was the Blood applied?"* I said, *"On the Mercy Seat"*. He replied; *"IT SPEAKS MERCY!"* We began to study *"mercy"* and discovered that mercy is much more than we had previously thought. Psalm 136 contains a powerful sevenfold definition of mercy giving us the key to properly worship the Lamb of God for His shed Blood!

Ps 136:1-4
O give thanks unto the LORD; for he is good: for his mercy endureth for ever. O give thanks unto the God of gods: for his mercy endureth for ever. O give thanks to the Lord of lords: for his mercy endureth for ever. To him who alone doeth great wonders: for his mercy endureth for ever.

In these verses we have the identity, the **TOTAL DOMINION**, and supremacy of God in His mercy. First the scripture tells us that He is good, and the God of gods and the Lord of lords. Then it declares His supremacy by saying He alone does great wonders. The goodness, dominion and supremacy of God and His mercy have no equal.

Ps 136:5-9
To him that by wisdom made the heavens: for his mercy endureth for ever. To him that stretched out the earth above the waters: for his mercy endureth for ever. To him that made great lights: for his mercy endureth for ever: The sun to rule by day: for his mercy endureth for ever: The moon and stars to rule by night: for his mercy endureth for ever.

In these scriptures we have the awesome **CREATIVE POWER** of His mercy. This power made the heavens, the earth, the stars, the sun and the moon! Isn't it interesting to know that mercy has the power to create?

Ps 136:10-12
To him that smote Egypt in their firstborn: for his mercy endureth for ever: And brought out Israel from among them: for his mercy endureth for ever: With a strong hand, and with a stretched out arm: for his mercy endureth for ever.

Mercy killed the first born of Egypt bringing **TOTAL DELIVERANCE**. What a contrast! First we have mercy identified as being good in God's total dominion and creative power. Now we see mercy delivering God's people from bondage! Glory to God!

Ps 136:13-16
To him which divided the Red sea into parts: for his mercy endureth for ever: And made Israel to pass through the midst of it: for his mercy endureth for ever: But overthrew Pharaoh and his host in the Red sea: for his mercy endureth for ever. To him which led his people through the wilderness: for his mercy endureth for ever.

MIRACULOUS POWER is in mercy! We see God opening the Red Sea for Israel to pass through. Then we see Pharaoh and his host destroyed. We also see that God led the Israelites through the wilderness, which was in itself a miraculous feat. Their food and water was supplied supernaturally and their clothing never wore out!

Ps 136:17-20
To him which smote great kings: for his mercy endureth for ever: And slew famous kings: for his mercy endureth for ever: Sihon king of the Amorites: for his mercy endureth for ever: And Og the king of Bashan: for his mercy endureth for ever:

Mercy **DESTROYS OUR ENEMIES!** Just as there are ranks in a physical army, there are ranks in the spiritual realm. Kings are the highest rank. *"Sihon king of the Amorites"* means a violent spirit with evil influence. *"Og king of Bashan"* denotes a demonic spirit of pride and arrogance. The mercy of God destroys these demonic influences over our lives.

Ps 136:21-22
And gave their land for an heritage: for his mercy endureth for ever: Even an heritage unto Israel his servant: for his mercy endureth for ever.

We have the manifestation of **COVENANT BLESSINGS** through His mercy. Mercy also gives us the power to rule with the authority of God. As we learned earlier the name *"Israel"* means to rule as God, and like Him we speak the Word and see it manifested. In essence mercy will bring the manifestation of covenant blessings and our spiritual inheritance.

Ps 136:23-26
Who remembered us in our low estate: for his mercy endureth for ever: And hath redeemed us from our enemies: for his mercy endureth for ever. Who giveth food to all flesh: for his mercy endureth for ever. O give thanks unto the God of heaven: for his mercy endureth for ever.

These scriptures highlight the **GRACE** that is in the mercy of God. First we are remembered in our low estate and are rescued from all our enemies. Then we find that mercy brings forth the provision for all of God's creation. This is truly unmerited favor, kindness, and compassion.

The mercy of God is sevenfold and it brings *dominion, creative power, deliverance, miracles, destruction of enemies, covenant blessings* and the *grace* of God. The mercies of God are outstanding and they are renewed every morning!

At the Mercy Seat we worship the Father, Son, and Holy Spirit for the sevenfold mercies of the Blood of Jesus. Now that we know what the Blood speaks on our behalf, we can come into agreement with it, and declare it in worship. As we do this we activate the awesome power of the Blood of Jesus in our lives! Worthy is the Lamb of God!

"Daddy" God

As we begin to worship the Blood upon the Mercy Seat, we begin to understand that the Blood is speaking total and complete restoration. Before the fall, Adam experienced perfect fellowship with the Father. The Blood upon the heavenly Mercy Seat has restored us to this perfection in fellowship. None of us had perfect earthly fathers. No matter how good they may have been, they could not be perfect. But our heavenly Father is the perfection of Fatherhood. In reality, the way we respond to our heavenly Father, in some ways, is affected by the relationship we have with our earthly fathers. That is why it is so important to have our minds renewed by the Word of God to separate the perception of our earthly fathers from our heavenly Father. Since we cannot know God apart from His Word, we have to allow the truth of the Word to build the true image of a father, our heavenly Father, within us. When that happens, there can be perfection in worship and fellowship!

When we come into the Holy of Holies, we understand that we are there because the Blood is speaking *"mercy"* on our behalf. As this realization sinks in, we will want to love our Daddy with all of our heart, soul, and mind. Every part of our being will sing songs of love and worship to Him.

Many times I see myself in His arms, with my head pressed against His chest. He wraps me in His arms like a warm blanket. I express my love to Him and I hear His heart of love for me. In the intimacy of our relationship, I cannot help but call Him *"Daddy"*. As I bask in His presence, I know that this is everything my heart has desired or ever will desire. This is truly the rest that I have been seeking all of my life. I am overwhelmed with gratitude to my Daddy for making it all possible. I worship Jesus, the Son, for His holy Blood and I worship the precious Holy Spirit for applying the Blood to my life. I worship the Father, Son, and Holy Spirit, uniquely and supremely worthy of all worship. My true heart's desire is to have everyone know and experience this unspeakable joy!

The Triune Anointing

Heb 9:3-5
And after the second veil, the tabernacle which is called the Holiest of all; which had the golden censer, and the ark of the covenant overlaid round about with gold, wherein was the golden pot that had manna, and Aaron's rod that budded, and the tables of the covenant; And over it the cherubims of glory shadowing the mercyseat; of which we cannot now speak particularly.

The Ark of the Covenant was a golden *"treasure"* chest that housed three items that were proof of the covenant promises God made to Israel. The first item was the Golden Pot of Manna representing how God supernaturally fed the Israelites in the wilderness with Manna from heaven. The second item was Aaron's rod that blossomed representing the power of a holy priesthood to bring about restoration. The third item was the Tables of the Law, which Moses received at Mount Sinai, representing the Word of God. These three items were symbolic of the offices of the king, priest and prophet. Jesus, the King-

Priest-Prophet, desires every believer to walk in this triune anointing.

The Golden Pot of Manna was symbolic of the office of the Prophet. **Jesus, the Prophet**, was the *"Bread of Life"* or *"True Manna"* for the world. We are to be His **prophets**, filled with Manna, feeding lost souls by proclaiming the Gospel to all men. The **Priesthood of Jesus** was found in the Rod of Aaron that miraculously brought forth buds, blossoms and fruit displaying resurrection power. Jesus, as the Priest of God, had resurrection power to raise the dead, heal all manner of disease, and cast out demons. As His **priests**, we are to bud, blossom and bear fruit with this same power through intercession and communion with God. The Tables of the Law represented the **Kingship of Jesus**. He was the Living Word, Who spoke the oracles of God. As His **kings,** we are to declare and decree the Word of God and establish it upon this earth, to manifest His awesome power and presence!

Chapter Eleven

The Tabernacle Prayer Pattern

Come And Take This Journey With Me!

Come And Take This Journey With Me!

I bring repentance and thanksgiving,
Entering in by the *"WAY"*
For the Blood You shed for my sins,
I am so thankful each and every day.
The light of day or natural light
Is available, allowing me to see;
The Blood You shed on Calvary, for the world,
And thank God just for me!

The Blood that speaks of better things
Than that of Abel, even now;
It calls to the world in earnest longings;
"My children, where art thou?"
Then I enter into *"TRUTH"*, Your Word
Having washed and set me apart;
To be illuminated by the Candlestick,
So that I can begin to know Your heart.

The Light of the world, brings the light of the Word,
And I will glorify Your name;
And I know that in this, I am marked for life
And I will never be the same.
There's complete satisfaction as I receive
The "Bread of Life"; Lord I understand the cost;
So I bear the world upon my shoulders and heart,
As I bring intercession for the lost.

As I enter into the veil called *"LIFE"*,
Where the veil of Your flesh was torn;
As I bring true worship in love to You,
To Your life and purpose, I'll conform.
I worship You in the beauty of holiness;
I'll give glory due Your name.
And as I give You glory, honor, and strength,
You'll bring the promises I have claimed.

I no longer need natural light or candlelight
To obtain the promises You have for me;
Because now I'm in Your presence,
And Your goodness and glory, now I see!
Praise God, I have entered into the realm,
Where the God in Christ; becomes Christ in me!
This ageless truth hidden from the prudent and wise;
That Christ in me; is the hope of glory!

I've partaken of the Heavenly Gift,
I am a carrier of Your presence this day.
With the Word of God in my heart;
To blossom in fruitfulness, is the only way.
As I learn to abide in, walk in; and live in
The overflow of Your glory;
The world will know that I've been with You;
And I will be sure and tell the story!

And I'll invite them all to come with me,
And know what I have been graced to see;
All it takes is the willingness of heart,
To come and take this journey with me!

Introduction To The Prayer Pattern

The building of the Tabernacle was for the purpose of God dwelling with His people. He gave His people a way to receive atonement for their sins and a method of approach to Him. Everything in the Tabernacle was a type and shadow of the life and ministry of the Lord Jesus Christ. As we have emphasized in this book, God's ultimate purpose is to have a nation of kings-priests to come into His holy presence and worship Him.

The Israelites rejected their king-priest calling, and desired Moses to speak to God for them. They did not want a personal relationship with God! This Prayer Pattern will give you the ability to have a personal relationship with God and fulfill your king-priest calling. While praying this Pattern your excitement will grow as you behold the glory of our Lord and Savior Jesus Christ in every phase of His life, death, resurrection, and glorification. As you declare the Word of God in these areas, you will begin to see the *"Word made flesh"* or the manifested glory of God in your life. You will realize, with more clarity, the power of the incorruptible seed of the Word of God to produce the Kingdom of God, in your life and the lives of others.

The front gate of the Tabernacle in the wilderness was called the *"WAY"*. In the courtyard or Outer Court was the Brazen Altar and Brazen Laver. There was also a gate to enter the Inner Court, called *"TRUTH"* and only the priests could enter beyond this point. In the Inner Court or Holy Place there was a Golden Candlestick, which illuminated everything. Next, there was the Table of Shewbread directly across from the

Candlestick and the Altar of Incense stood in front of the veil leading to the Holy of Holies. The veil, which was called the *"LIFE"*, guarded the entrance into the Most Holy Place or Holy of Holies, where the Ark of the Covenant stood. God's glory *(Shekinah)* dwelt there above the Mercy Seat upon the Ark. Only the High Priest was allowed to go beyond the veil. He was permitted to do this once a year, on the Day of Atonement, to offer the blood of the sacrifice for the sins of the people. When Jesus said in John 14:6, *"I am the way, the truth, and the life: no man cometh unto the Father, but by me,"* the Jews knew exactly what He meant. He was, in effect saying, **"I Am the Tabernacle, the only access to the presence of God the Father"**.

The Lord Jesus Christ is the fulfillment of the types and shadows in the Tabernacle. We must enter into the **Gate**, if we hope to find eternal life. We must also repent and accept Jesus Christ as our Lord and Savior, acknowledging Him as the Lamb of God slain on the Brazen Altar of Calvary.

After we have received salvation, we begin our prayer journey by repenting and then entering His gates with thanksgiving. At the **Brazen Altar** we daily acknowledge the power of the Lord's shed Blood. The **Brazen Laver** symbolizes the cleansing power of God's Eternal Word. This is where we are washed by the water of the *"Word"*, Who is the Lord Jesus. The **Golden Candlestick** illuminates and reveals the power of the Lord Jesus Christ and the ministry of the Holy Spirit in our lives. The **Table of Shewbread** represents the four corners of the earth and the people for which the Lord died. It is here that we enter our role as intercessors and intercede for those people who are on God's heart. The **Altar of Incense** represents *"true worship"* and it is here that we worship Him in spirit and in truth. This is the final step of the purging process that will allow us to go beyond the veil and enter into God's presence.

When Jesus died on Calvary, the veil of the Temple was rent in two, signifying that the most important step in life is to come beyond that veil into the Holy of Holies. In the Holy of Holies, stood the **Ark of the Covenant**, which housed the Tables of the Law, the Golden Pot of Manna, and Aaron's Rod. Jesus, the King-Priest-Prophet, was the Ark of God! It is God's desire that we become like the Ark, carriers of the presence of God with Christ in us, the hope of glory!

Many Christians stay in the Outer Court, or the Inner Court in their relationship with the Lord. They can still experience blessing, because the radius of God's presence is so great. But the fullness of blessing can only be realized by entering into the Most Holy Place, and into the arms of our loving *"Daddy"*. Our *"Daddy"* desires that we don't spend our time in the Outer or Inner Court. He is calling us to a face-to-face relationship with Him in the glory realm. Praise God; let's answer that call! Dear Saints, in this realm, you have the manifested Word of God, His glory, and His goodness. You will see your life changed and enriched in such a marvelous way and it is our desire to show you how to do it. This portion is not intended to be an exhaustive study on the Tabernacle. There are many great books that are available on this subject. This section is simply presenting you with our Pattern for prayer and fellowship with God. We have also included the correlation of each section to the Lord's Prayer (Matthew 6:9-13).

As you begin to pray according to Pattern, you will be cleansed, purged, and will realize the importance of your calling as king-priest intercessor. You will notice the growth in your spirit-man because praying this Pattern is establishing the Word of God in your life. It is essential to understand that there is no greater force in the universe than the Word of God. The angels or ministering spirits hearken unto the voice of His Word, not your opinions or ability to speak well, so ***please pray the Word of God!*** You will be empowered and learn how to bring *"true worship"* by worshipping the Father, Son, and Holy Spirit, in a new realm and with new revelation. So ***"Come And Take This Journey With Me!"*** If you have not received Jesus Christ as your personal Lord and Savior, this is where you must begin. Please confess the following prayer out loud:

Dear Heavenly Father,

I come to You in the name of the Lord Jesus Christ. I repent of my sins and I ask for Your forgiveness. I now confess that Jesus is my Lord and Savior and I believe in my heart that He died for me and was raised from the dead. I ask You Jesus to come into my heart and live Your life through me. At this moment I believe that I am born again by an act of Your love, grace and mercy. Thank You for saving my soul. Amen.

Rom 10:9-10
That if thou shalt confess with thy mouth the Lord Jesus, and shalt believe in thine heart that God hath raised him from the dead, thou shalt be saved. For with the heart man believeth unto righteousness; and with the mouth confession is made unto salvation.

Tips On Praying The Pattern

The Pattern is the most important aspect of the prayer **NOT OUR CHOICE** of scriptures, so please feel free to use your own favorite scriptures that apply. The Word of God is inexhaustible so you can change often. However, even if you use the same scriptures, the revelation that God gives and the fellowship that you will experience will make it different each time. Use your Bible during prayer, or write your scriptures out. God is not concerned with whether you know them by heart or not. The important thing is that you are declaring the Word of God in divine order.

The Pattern consists of three extremely vital stages that must be adhered to in order to be effective and get into the Secret Place of the Most High.

- The first stage is where you repent of your own sins.
- The second stage is where you are anointed and equipped to stand in the gap, repent and intercede for all men.
- The third stage is where you purge your heart and become a true worshipper unto the Lord and enter into His presence.

One cannot rightfully go beyond the veil into the presence of God, unless these things are taken care of first. Please understand that we are not saying that you have never been in the presence of God in prayer. All of us have gotten there on occasion, without this Pattern. Those are the times that we cherish and remember as special prayer times. Those special prayer times happened basically by one of these three conditions: The grace of God, the Holy Spirit getting us there by the power of tongues, or an anointed servant of the Lord taking us there. There is absolutely nothing wrong with any of these ways, however they do not give us revelation knowledge on how to return when we desire. God wants us to mature to the point, where we know how to get into His presence.

As mentioned earlier, the radius of God presence will bring great blessing in the Outer or Inner Courts, but you have not lived until you have experienced His presence beyond the veil! This is now available every time you pray, not just periodically. When you step out in faith and begin to worship the Lord in this fashion you will feel the presence of the Holy Spirit. It is His job to glorify Jesus and to bring you into all truth (John 16:13-14). Jesus also said the Comforter would teach you all things, and bring to your remembrance all things He has said! So just yield to Him and you will be amazed at how powerful your prayer time will become.

Do not concern yourself with the time element. God is so great in manifold wisdom that this type of prayer can be completed in one minute, or it can be transformed into an all night vigil. This prayer usually takes about fifteen minutes. You can also alternate praying the steps of the Pattern with a prayer partner---or each person in a group can pray a segment of the Pattern to complete the prayer. You can do it anywhere or at anytime. As long as you do it according to Pattern you will experience the awesome presence of God!

Other Suggestions:

- *Record yourself reading the full Prayer Pattern. You will be amazed at hearing how powerful you sound praying the Word of God.*
- *Play your recorded prayer often and pray along with it to get it into your spirit.*
- *Do not quote scripture references in the Prayer Pattern that are within parenthesis.*
- *Utilize the Short Prayer for quick access to God's presence.*
- *We also encourage you to create your own short prayer using the model at the end of this chapter. When you become comfortable with praying it, continue to add scriptures to grow your prayer.*
- *Always bind Psalms 91 to everyone after completing major warfare.*
- *Last but not least, enhance your prayer even further by using God's Jewish Names. He loves it! Jesus can be referred to as Yeshua (Our Salvation) or Yahshua (Our God is our Salvation). The Holy Spirit can be referred to as the Ruach HaKodesh and God the Father as YHVH or Yahweh!*

Daily Performing
Your King-Priest Ministry

In this chapter we will explain each section of the Tabernacle, its furnishings and their fulfillment in the Lord Jesus Christ. We will also combine the Lord's Prayer and scriptures into a prayer for that section. This will give you a complete understanding of the Prayer Pattern.

Heb 8:5
Who serve unto the example and shadow of heavenly things, as Moses was admonished of God when he was about to make the Tabernacle: for, See, saith he, that thou make all things ACCORDING TO THE PATTERN shewed to thee in the mount.

In Hebrews 8:5, we see that the Tabernacle of Moses was made according to divine order. It was a type and shadow of the heavenly Tabernacle, and foreshadowed the life and ministry of the Lord Jesus Christ. It is also our Prayer Pattern or method of approach into the presence of God.

Brass is found in the Outer Court denoting judgment; silver is found in the Inner Court symbolizing redemption, and gold is found in the Holy of Holies representing Divinity. We are not to spend our prayer time in the Outer or Inner Courts, but we are to go directly into the Holy of Holies—in other words, we are to **"GO FOR THE GOLD"!**

The Outer Court

The Outer Court consisted of the Brazen Altar of Sacrifice and the Brazen Laver. Brass denotes judgment against sin. Our sin is judged in the Outer Court by two elements, the Blood of Jesus and the water of the Word of God. These two elements are shown in John 19:34, where the soldier pierced the side of Jesus bringing forth Blood and water. First the Blood redeems us, and then we are cleansed by the water of the Word.

Also according to Isaiah 4:4, the *"spirit of judgment and the spirit of burning"* will purge us, therefore making it possible for God to *"Tabernacle"* among us. The Spirit of Judgment and Burning is the Holy Spirit. He convicts us of our sin and judges it on the cross of Calvary. He then applies the Blood of Jesus to our lives and purifies us with His holy fire. The Outer Court had the natural sunlight, while the Inner Court (Holy Place) had candlelight and the Holy of Holies had the light of God's glory. The Outer Court was available to all by simply entering the gate, symbolizing that salvation is for everyone (John 3:16). But before we can enter our priesthood our sin must be taken care of in the Outer Court.

First Confess Your Sins And Repent

We must first confess and repent of our sins and release others in forgiveness. If we regard iniquity in our hearts, the Lord will not hear us (Psalms 66:18).

Prayer:
1. *The Gate – Repentance*
FATHER I REPENT AND CONFESS MY SINS.

Father, have mercy upon me according to Your loving kindness and tender mercies and blot out my transgressions. Wash me from iniquity and cleanse me from sin. For against You and You only I have sinned **(Ps 51:1-4)**. Father in the name of Jesus, I repent for every sin known, unknown, omitted, and committed. I repent for unforgiveness and I release and forgive all **(Mark 11:25)**. I ask You to cleanse me from secret faults and keep me back from presumptuous sins; and let them not have dominion over me: then I shall be upright, and innocent from the great transgression **(Ps 19:12-13).** Father, I thank You that Your Word says in **I John 1:9,** If I confess my sins, You are faithful and just to forgive me, and to cleanse me from all unrighteousness. Create in me a clean heart and renew a right spirit within me and let the words of my mouth and the meditation of my heart be acceptable in Your sight O Lord my strength and Redeemer **(Ps 51:10) -- (Ps 19:14).**

Entering The Gate

After repentance, we begin at the linen gate surrounding the courtyard. As Psalms 100 states, we enter into this gate, called the WAY, with thanksgiving. Thanksgiving is a response to the goodness of God, which embraces His kindness, favor and compassion. This gate was the only entrance to the Tabernacle. It was facing the east and the rising sun. This speaks of a new day dawning with brightness and hope. Those that want to approach God can do so only one way, in the *"light"* of the glorious gospel of the Lord Jesus Christ.

Ex 27:16
And for the gate of the court shall be an hanging of twenty cubits, of blue, and purple, and scarlet, and fine twined linen, wrought with needlework: and their pillars shall be four, and their sockets four.

This gate, the *"WAY"*, was low and wide (20 cubits wide by 5 cubits high). God so loved the world that He gave His only begotten Son, so that whosoever desires to come to Him, may come. The dimensions for the gate called *"TRUTH"* were 10 by 10 cubits. This entrance to the Holy Place was for the priesthood only. The dimensions for the entrance into the Holy of Holies, the *"LIFE"*, were also 10 by 10 cubits. The entrances to the *"TRUTH"* and *"LIFE"* were narrower, than the *"WAY"*. Sadly, there are those who receive salvation but do not continue the journey into the presence of God. However, if we choose to go beyond the *"TRUTH"* and the *"LIFE"*, we will find *"zoe"* life or the *"GOD-KIND OF LIFE"* (Matthew 7:13-14).

Our Father Which Art In Heaven, Hallowed Be Thy Name
(Matt 6:9)

Our Lord Jesus revealed God to us as our Father. We respond with thanksgiving for the goodness and favor of God. We begin to praise, exalt, and extol the name of the Lord. We can thank Him with scripture declaring the power, strength, and majesty of His name. Once we have hallowed or consecrated His name, we have established our foundation for thanksgiving, praise, and worship, throughout the Tabernacle.

Prayer:
The Gate – Thanksgiving
FATHER I ENTER YOUR GATES WITH THANKSGIVING.
[Our Father Which Art In Heaven, Hallowed Be Thy Name]

Father I praise You, hallow Your holy name, and thank You for Your love. Lord I praise You for Your mighty acts and I praise You according to Your excellent greatness. Let everything that has breath praise the Lord **(Ps 150:1-2,6).**

O Lord, my Lord how excellent is Your name in all the earth **(Ps 8:1)**! The name of the Lord is a strong tower and the righteous run into it and are safe **(Prov 18:10)**. O magnify the Lord with me, and let's exalt His name together **(Ps 34:3)**. The Lord's name is to be praised from the rising of the sun to the going down of the same **(Ps 113:3)**. Every day I will bless You Lord, and I will praise Your name forever and ever **(Ps 145:2)**.

The Brazen Altar

Ex 27:1-3
And thou shalt make an altar of shittim wood, five cubits long, and five cubits broad; the altar shall be foursquare: and the height thereof shall be three cubits. And thou shalt make the horns of it upon the four corners thereof: his horns shall be of the same: and thou shalt overlay it with brass. And thou shalt make his pans to receive his ashes, and his shovels, and his basons, and his fleshhooks, and his firepans: all the vessels thereof thou shalt make of brass.

The first piece of furniture we encounter on our journey is the Brazen Altar of Sacrifice. An altar is a platform or elevated place used for sacrifice. The Brazen Altar was made of acacia wood, which was non-decaying and non-corruptible. It was overlaid with brass within and without. Brass is the symbol of judgment against sin. This is the place where the animals were sacrificed to make atonement for the sins of the Israelites.

For atonement, the death of an *"innocent"* victim was required. The shedding of blood began in Genesis 3:21. God *"covered"* the sin of Adam and Eve by killing an innocent animal, thereby providing an atonement as well as clothing. Leviticus 17:11 states, *"the life of the flesh is in the blood; I have given it to you upon the altar to make an atonement for your souls"*. Jesus gave His life as a Lamb without spot or blemish on Calvary, His Altar of Sacrifice. Yes, Calvary is the fulfillment of the Brazen Altar of Sacrifice, where the Lamb of God was slain for the sins of the world. This is where we express a true heart recognition and appreciation for the Blood that Jesus shed for our salvation.

Jesus Our Mighty Conquering Hero!

Col 2:14-15
Blotting out the handwriting of ordinances that was against us, which was contrary to us, and took it out of the way, nailing it to his cross; And having spoiled principalities and powers, he made a shew of them openly, triumphing over them in it.

The word *"blotting"* means to smear out, obliterate, erase tears, and pardon sin. It also means removing, loosing, and putting away sin. The *"handwriting of ordinances"* was a legal document pronouncing us guilty and worthy of death. Verse 14 states that Jesus *"took it out of the way"* and erased the guilty verdict by nailing it to His cross! Verse 15 states, that *"he spoiled principalities and powers and made a shew of them openly"*!

The Greek definitions reflect a picture of a conquering hero who strips his defeated foe of all of his weapons. While he is standing naked of power, he is led off as a captive and paraded openly in total humiliation. This is what Jesus did to satan and his demons! Psalms 24 gives us the picture of the victory celebration in heaven. Our Lord is hailed and exalted as the Lord strong and mighty and the Lord mighty in battle returning with the spoils of this victory! God the Father exalted Jesus and gave Him the keys of hell and of death according to Revelation 1:18.   He also gave Him a position *"far above all principality, and power, and might, and dominion, and every name that is named, not only in this world, but also in that which is to come: And hath put all things under his feet and gave him to be the head over all things to the church"* (Ephesians 1:21-22). Praise His Wonderful Name!

The Priests Were Anointed With Blood

The blood of the sacrifice was the foundation of the Tabernacle of Moses and the only foundation for worship and fellowship with God. Likewise, Christianity is based upon the foundation of the Blood of Jesus Christ. In the Tabernacle the blood was sprinkled upon everything, including the priests.

Lev 8:23-24
And he slew it; and Moses took of the blood of it, and put it upon the tip of Aaron's right ear, and upon the thumb of his right hand, and upon the great toe of his right foot. And he brought Aaron's sons, and Moses put of the blood upon the tip of their right ear, and upon the thumbs of their right hands, and upon the great toes of their right feet: and Moses sprinkled the blood upon the altar round about.

We can ask the Lord to anoint us so that we can minister unto Him. When we pray, we ask God to anoint our right ear with the Blood of Jesus, so we can hear what the Spirit is saying unto us. We ask Him to anoint our right thumb for *"our hands to war and our fingers to fight"*. We also ask Him to anoint our right toe, so we can walk in His ways and receive the anointing to crush the enemy under our feet. As king-priests, we should recognize the power of the Blood of Jesus in every realm. The blood was sprinkled upon everything in the Tabernacle, from the front gate to the Holy of Holies. Therefore, our prayer in the Pattern of the Tabernacle is based upon the Blood of Jesus.

The Voice Of The Blood

When Adam sinned, God felt that separation, and He called to Adam *"where art thou?"* The voice of God calls out from the Blood of Jesus in earnest longings to a lost and dying world, *"where art thou?"* The Blood is speaking redemption to the unsaved; while at the same time it is calling out to Christians to enter into God's presence as king-priests. Revelation 5:9-10 declares that Jesus redeemed us by His Blood, and made us kings and priests unto our God to rule and reign on this earth.

In summary, God came out of His throne room, stepping out of eternity into time, to be born as a man. He proceeded to fulfill the Law of God by living a sinless life. He accomplished the travail of His soul in the *"Garden of Gethsemane"* and continued to the *"Brazen Altar of Calvary"* to be our *"holy sin offering"*. He then became the *"scapegoat"* for our sins and took them to hell. After three days He arose victorious over death, hell, and the grave. In Revelation 1:18, Jesus declares that He lives and was dead, and is alive for evermore; and has the keys of hell and death. Hallelujah! He is the Lord of Hosts, the Lord strong and mighty, and the King of glory, victorious over all of His enemies!

Thy Kingdom Come
(Matt 6:10)

When we thank God for the Blood of Jesus, we are praising Him that His Kingdom has come to earth, by way of the Lord Jesus Christ. He came to establish the Kingdom of God on earth, which is His rule, reign, dominion and order of doing things. Adam's original mandate was to subdue the earth, through God's power and dominion. Jesus came as the last Adam, to restore us to that original state. The Kingdom of God can only be established on this earth, as we recognize the power and authority of the Blood of Jesus in our daily lives.

Prayer:
2. *The Brazen Altar*
FATHER THANK YOU FOR THE BLOOD OF JESUS CHRIST.
[Thy Kingdom Come]

Father, thank You for loving me so much that You gave Your only begotten Son, that whosoever shall believe in Him should not perish but have everlasting life **(John 3:16).** He was wounded for my transgressions, He was bruised for my iniquities: the chastisement of my peace was upon Him; and with His stripes I am healed **(Isa 53:5).** Thank You Lord Jesus for blotting out the handwriting of the ordinances that were against me and taking them out of the way by nailing them to Your cross. In the process You defeated and triumphed over every evil power and made a show of them openly **(Col 2:14-15).** Father God, I thank You for the precious Blood of Jesus that was shed for the remission of all my sins. I plead and apply the Blood of Jesus to every part of my life and upon every precious stone in my breastplate. **Gal 3:13** assures me that Christ has redeemed me from every curse over my life, that I may partake of the blessings of Abraham. Thank You Lord Jesus for redeeming me by Your Blood and making me a

king-priest unto God to reign on this earth **(Rev 5:9-10).**
Father I thank You that Your kingdom has come in my life.

The Brazen Laver

Ex 30:18-21
Thou shalt also make a laver of brass, and his foot also of brass, to wash withal: and thou shalt put it between the tabernacle of the congregation and the altar, and thou shalt put water therein. For Aaron and his sons shall wash their hands and their feet thereat: When they go into the tabernacle of the congregation, THEY SHALL WASH WITH WATER, THAT THEY DIE NOT; OR WHEN THEY COME NEAR TO THE ALTAR TO MINISTER, to burn offering made by fire unto the LORD: So they shall wash their hands and their feet, that they die not: and it shall be a statute for ever to them, even to him and to his seed throughout their generations.

The second piece of furniture in the Outer Court was the Brazen Laver and it was filled with water. The priests would wash their hands and feet at this Laver before performing their priestly duties. The first time Aaron and His sons were washed, the washing was done for them by another (Moses), as stated in Exodus 29:4. This is a type of our new birth where the Lord washed and redeemed us from the original sin of Adam. The water also symbolized the cleansing power of the Word of God. Notice that after the initial washing, it was then the responsibility of the priests to wash themselves before performing ANY priestly duties in the Tabernacle. They were to wash their hands and feet, their WORKS and their WALK.

Before we minister unto the Lord in prayer, we should wash ourselves with the Word of repentance. Ephesians 5:26-27 states: *"That he might sanctify and cleanse it with the washing of water by the word, That he might present it to himself a glorious church, not having spot, or wrinkle, or any such thing; but that it should be holy and without blemish"*.

In John 13:5, we see a demonstration of the Lord Jesus performing this washing when He washed the feet of His disciples. They were washed with the water by the Word! The Lord also prayed in John 17:17, that we would be sanctified or *"set apart"* by the truth of the Word of God. As the Word separates us from the world unto God, we can then find our unique place in the plans and purposes of God. We cannot go forward into our king-priest calling without being washed with the water by the Word.

Be A Doer Of The Word

According to Exodus 38:8, the Laver had mirrors in it. James 1:22-25, tells us that the Word of God must be applied to our lives. We must look into the Laver of God's Word, as we would a mirror, and wash ourselves with it. We are to look into the Word, see our condition versus what God says about us, and make a decision to walk in His truth. We are not to forget what we see, hear, or what *"manner of man"* we are. But we are to continue in the perfect law of liberty. There are two laws at work on this earth. We, as Christians, can choose which law we will live under. According to Romans 8:2, there is the *"law of sin and death"*, and there is the *"law of the Spirit of life in Christ Jesus"*. Whichever law we choose to live under will determine our effectiveness in this life. In order to live under the *"law of the spirit of life in Christ Jesus"*, we must say what the Word of God says about us. We must declare Who He is, and who we are in Him.

Remember the Tabernacle of Moses is also called the *"Tabernacle of Testimony"*. We overcome by the Blood of the Lamb and the word of our testimony. Our testimony of the life, death, resurrection, and glorification of the Lord Jesus Christ will lead us to victory. We operate in our calling as king-priests when we declare the Word of God. According to Hebrews 3:1, Jesus is the Apostle and High Priest of our profession or confession. Therefore, He is anointed to bring every word to pass that we speak, WHEN we speak His Word!

Thy Will Be Done
(Matt 6:10)

The Word of God is the will of God. Therefore when we pray the Word, we are declaring: "Thy will be done". Psalms 119:89 states, "For ever, O LORD, thy word is settled in heaven". The Word of God is settled in heaven, and the only way to settle it on earth is for us to pray or speak it.

Prayer:
3. The Brazen Laver
FATHER THANK YOU FOR YOUR WORD.
[Thy Will Be Done]

Father, I thank You that **John 1:1** says, in the beginning was the Word, and the Word was with God, and the Word was God. **John 1:14** says that the Word was made flesh, and dwelt among us, (and we beheld

His glory, the glory of the only begotten of the Father), full of grace and truth. Jesus is the Word made flesh. Your Word is made flesh or manifested in my life, as I establish Your Word upon this earth. Your Word is health and healing to all of my flesh **(Prov 4:22)**. Your Word is quick and powerful and sharper than any two-edged sword and is able to divide the soul and spirit, the joints and marrow, and discern the thoughts and intents of the heart **(Heb 4:12)**. Your Word is a lamp unto my feet, and a light unto my path **(Ps 119:105)**. I receive the blessings of **Deut 28:1-14**, because I hearken diligently unto Your Word. I thank You Father that I have been sanctified and cleansed with the washing of water by the Word of God **(Eph 5:26)**. Your Word is Your will, therefore let Your will be done in my life.

The Holy Place

I Peter 2:9
But ye are a chosen generation, a royal priesthood, an holy nation, a peculiar people; that ye should shew forth the praises of him who hath called you out of darkness into his marvellous light:

Leaving the Outer Court, the priests would enter into the Holy Place. The Holy Place is where the Candlestick, the Table of Shewbread and the Altar of Incense were housed. The Holy Place was only for the priests. In order to enter in, you had to be *"born"* into the priesthood. It is the same today; you cannot enter into the Holy Place unless you have been *"born-again"* and desire to fulfill your calling to the priesthood.

The curtain that separated the Outer Court from the Holy Place was called *"TRUTH"*. In order to enter in, there must be a more intense desire concerning the purposes of God, beyond receiving salvation. Many Christians choose not to go beyond the Outer Court. It is so sad because the richness and fullness they are seeking in their relationship with the Lord can only be found in continuing the journey into His presence. The *"TRUTH"* was held in place by five columns, symbolic of the five-fold ministry according to Ephesians 4:11. These columns also represent grace and the five anointings that each believer is to walk in. These anointings, supplied by the Holy Spirit, are apostolic, prophetic, evangelistic, pastoral and teaching. We should be equipped to minister in any capacity to meet the need. It is only after we have traveled beyond the gate of *"TRUTH"*, that we begin to understand the higher purposes of God and these anointings. This is the place where we begin to share a more intimate relationship with the Lord, and He begins to reveal His true character and nature. Being in relationship with God is a blessing that is beyond any earthly treasure!

The Golden Candlestick

Ex 25:31-32
And thou shalt make a candlestick of pure gold: of beaten work shall the candlestick be made: his shaft, and his branches, his bowls, his knops, and his flowers, shall be of the same. And six branches shall come out of the sides of it; three branches of the candlestick out of the one side, and three branches of the candlestick out of the other side:

The Golden Candlestick is the third piece of furniture that we encounter on our journey. The Candlestick was made of pure gold, consisting of a center branch, and six other branches proceeding from the center branch. Each branch had a lamp containing pure olive oil, and was to be kept burning continually. It was the only light in the Holy Place and illuminated everything. Jesus said in John 8:12; *"I am the light of the world: he that followeth me shall not walk in darkness, but shall have the light of life"*. The *"light of life"* that is promised to those who follow Him is the *"glory of God!"* In Matthew 5:14-16, Jesus declares that we are the light of the world and partakers of the glory of God. The light or glory will be so evident, that those in darkness will see our good works and glorify our Heavenly Father.

We should remember it was the continual supply of oil that brought forth the light (Exodus 27:20). We must spend time in God's presence daily to receive our fresh refilling or supply of oil. We should ask the Lord for His correction, or trimming of our wicks. We want to be that Candlestick, burning brightly and reflecting divine light. Also according to Exodus 25:31, the Candlestick, like our Savior, was hammered and beaten. But notice that the hammering yielded beautiful resurrection life in the form of buds, blossoms, and fruit.

The Lord Jesus Christ was beaten and crucified that we might experience *"new"* life in Him. There were seven branches in the Candlestick denoting the perfection of the sevenfold anointing as described in Isaiah 11:2. The Lord Jesus Christ embodied the sevenfold Spirit of God and according to Acts 10:38 and I John 3:8, Jesus was anointed with the Holy Ghost and power to heal the oppressed and to destroy the works of the devil. We are also anointed with the Holy Ghost and power, and will be that Lampstand burning brightly to duplicate Christ's ministry in the earth.

In Earth, As It Is In Heaven
(Matt 6:10)

As we thank God for the anointing of the Holy Spirit, we activate His power in our lives. He is the Comforter and the Spirit of Truth, Who was sent to manifest the glory of heaven on this earth.

Prayer:
4. The Golden Candlestick

FATHER THANK YOU FOR THE ANOINTING OF THE HOLY SPIRIT.

[In Earth, As It Is In Heaven]

In **John 8:12** Jesus said, I am the Light of the world and he that follows Me shall not walk in darkness but shall have the light of life. Father thank You for the *"light of life"*, which is the anointing. Jesus is the "Light of the world" and He has caused me to be a reflector of that light which will bring glory to my Heavenly Father **(Matt 5:14-16)**. **Acts 10:38** states, that God anointed Jesus of Nazareth with the Holy Ghost and with power: who went about doing good, and healing all that were oppressed of the devil; for God was with Him. I am also anointed with the Holy Spirit and I am born of God for the purpose of destroying the works of darkness **(I John 3:8)**. Jesus said in **John 14:12,** he that believes on Me, the works that I do he shall do also, and greater works than these. Thank You Lord for the anointing and the gifts of the Holy Spirit to do these greater works. I ask You Holy Spirit to flow through me as You purpose with the gift of faith, gifts of healing, working of miracles, word of wisdom, word of knowledge, discerning of spirits, tongues, interpretation of tongues, and prophecy **(I Cor 12:8-10).** I have the sevenfold anointing; the Spirit of the Lord, the spirit of wisdom and understanding, the spirit of counsel and might, the spirit of knowledge, and of the fear of the Lord **(Isa 11:2).** Father, correct me, so that nothing will hinder Your power from flowing through me and I can bring forth pure and holy light. Father, I thank You for the Holy Spirit, Who brings forth Your power from heaven. I also thank You for allowing me to share Your light all over this world.

The Table Of Shewbread

Ex 25:23-24,30
Thou shalt also make a table of shittim wood: two cubits shall be the length thereof, and a cubit the breadth thereof, and a cubit and a half the height thereof. And thou shalt overlay it with pure gold, and make thereto a crown of gold round about. And thou shalt set upon the table shewbread before me alway.

The Shewbread

In the Old Testament this Table was for the priests of the Lord. Now it is the Table of the redeemed of the Lord, His royal priesthood (I Peter 2:9). There were twelve loaves of bread, symbolic of the twelve tribes of Israel only, but now they represent the entire world. The loaves of bread were perforated and sprinkled with frankincense. Every Sabbath the bread was replaced, and the preceding bread was given to the priests for food. When translating *"bread"*, as stated before, it gives us the ability to war, battle, prevail, overcome, and be delivered. This Table also stood before the Lord, as a constant reminder of His love for His people. The words *"bread or shewbread"* also mean the *"presence bread"* or *"bread of faces"*. It was always in the Father's presence and continually before His face. The nation of Israel and the world are always on God's heart. We are loved and *"accepted in the beloved"*. We experience communion and sweet fellowship with God at this Table. The golden crown around the Table of Shewbread kept the bread from falling. This is a picture of Jude 24, which says that God is *"able to keep you from falling, and to present you faultless before the presence of his glory with exceeding joy"*.

The Wine

The drink offering consisted of wine that was poured out as an offering unto the Lord. The priests were not to drink it according to Numbers 28:7. The wine was symbolic of the *"cup of blessing"* that the Lord Jesus poured out in the Garden of Gethsemane. The priests were not allowed to drink the wine, which was symbolic of the Lord's Blood, BECAUSE HE HAD NOT YET COME. But as New Testament king-priests, we are told by Jesus to eat His flesh and drink His Blood (Matthew 26:26-28). This is the communion of the Lord's Table.

The Father's Heart

The Table of Shewbread had four corners, representing the four corners of the earth. God's entire reason for the plan of redemption was to bring His family home. It bears repeating, that the Father's eyes always rested on this Table. Therefore, we must understand the importance of the great commission (Mark 16:15). We should always be mindful to pray that God will raise up laborers to reap His harvest of children.

(Step 1) - Repentance For All

The first thing we do at the Table of Shewbread is stand in the gap and repent for the unsaved, world leadership, the Body of Christ and the nation of Israel (Ezekiel 22:30). The names of the twelve tribes of Israel were inscribed on stones, which were worn on the shoulders of the High priest. He also had the stones representing the twelve tribes on his breastplate. In the spirit realm, we wear a breastplate also. Now these names and stones represent physical Israel, the Body of Christ, the unsaved, and world leadership. We, as king-priests of the Lord, are to pray that the world will be reconciled to Him.

We intercede or stand in the gap for them according to Ezekiel 22:30 and repent for them according to Daniel 9, Ezra 9, and II Chronicles 7:14. In our king-priest calling, it is powerful when we follow the examples of Daniel, Ezra, and Solomon, and repent for our fellowman. God wants to bring blessing, not judgment, but how can He bless those that are wayward, in rebellion, and living in sin? The answer is that He cannot. But we, as king-priests of the Lord, can stand in the gap and repent for them and declare the Word of God over their lives. When this is done, the Holy Spirit will work with them to bring them to a personal repentance and knowledge of the Lord.

Daniel 9:5 shows Daniel, as the perfect intercessor, identifying with the sins of his nation and asking for mercy and forgiveness. We, as born-again believers, have the ministry of reconciliation and the word of reconciliation according to II Corinthians 5:18-19. We are to use this ministry to reconcile all men unto God. Please note that, at this point in the Prayer Pattern it becomes plural even if we are praying as an individual. We become intercessors that identify with the sins of the world and repent for them.

Daniel's Prayer Of Repentance

Dan 9:5
WE HAVE SINNED, AND HAVE COMMITTED INIQUITY, AND HAVE DONE WICKEDLY, *and have rebelled, even by departing from thy precepts and from thy judgments:*

Dan 9:19
O LORD, HEAR; O LORD, FORGIVE; O Lord, hearken and do; defer not, for thine own sake, O my God: for thy city and thy people are called by thy name.

(Step 2) - Spiritually Partake Of Communion

This Table also represents the Lord as the *"Bread of Life"* (John 6:48). Therefore in prayer, we spiritually partake of the Bread and Wine, which brings life to every form of death in our lives. This *"Bread and Wine"* which God provided, gives us the ability to destroy our enemies and bring deliverance to all men. After spiritually partaking of the broken body and shed Blood of our Lord Jesus Christ, we understand that we have a Blood-bought covenant right to intercede and to be heard!

(Step 3) - Put On The Whole Armor Of God

We must be equipped and prepared to do battle for the people that God has placed on our hearts and shoulders. We are to put on the whole armor of God according to Ephesians 6:10-18. Whether we know it or not, when we open our mouths to do warfare, we are on the battlefield. It is spiritual suicide to enter the battlefield without the armor of God!

(Step 4) – Spiritual Warfare

We bind and break the power of the strong man and demonic forces, then loose the angels with the Word of God for our situation. It is important to bind the strong man because he is the ruler over the demonic stronghold. When we bind him, then we are able to destroy his power (Matthew 12:29). A major part of our covenant blessings involve the ministry of angels. The first chapter of Hebrews tells us that they are ministering spirits FOR THE HEIRS OF SALVATION. We have awesome power at our disposal, but we must speak the Word. The angels do not hearken to our opinions or our own words they heed only the voice of God's Word. This means we must speak the Word of God, giving voice to it over every situation so the angels will have the necessary power to bring the victory (Psalms 103:20). We also need to pray with our Bibles open so the Lord can quicken different scriptures to us that need to be sown into the earth realm.

(Step 5) - Pray For The Unsaved, World Leadership, Body Of Christ, And Israel

We can now pray for and declare over every precious stone in our breastplates, the unsaved, leadership, Body of Christ and Israel. Constant prayer to the Lord of the Harvest should be made for the unsaved (Matthew 9:37-38). We are also told to make intercession for those in authority so that they may be saved and the gospel will have free course in the earth (I Timothy 2:1-4). And we, the Body of Christ, are encouraged to pray one for another (James 5:16-17).

The prayers of the Apostle Paul in Ephesians 1:17-23 and 3:14-21 are perfect prayers to bring about the glorification and perfection of the Church. Not only do they include wisdom and revelation for us to know the hope of His calling, but they also declare we have the resurrection power of Christ within us. These prayers also bring us to the point of knowing and understanding the love of God, so we can be filled with all the fullness of Christ.

Eph 1:17-18
That the God of our Lord Jesus Christ, the Father of glory, may give unto you the spirit of wisdom and revelation in the knowledge of him: The eyes of your understanding being enlightened; that ye may know what is the hope of his calling, and what the riches of the glory of his inheritance in the saints,

Eph 3:14-19
For this cause I bow my knees unto the Father of our Lord Jesus Christ, Of whom the whole family in heaven and earth is named, That he would grant you, according to the riches of his glory, to be strengthened with might by his Spirit in the inner man; That Christ may dwell in your hearts by faith; that ye, being rooted and grounded in

love, may be able to comprehend with all the saints what is the width and length and depth and height—to know the love of Christ which passes knowledge; that you may be filled with all the fullness of God.

In regard to Israel, we should delight in praying for the peace of Jerusalem because God's end-time plans and purposes will be fulfilled in the nation of Israel. In essence, when we pray for the peace of Jerusalem, we are praying for the return of the Lord Jesus Christ! In addition, we have been adopted by God and grafted into His Jewish family. Therefore, we have an obligation to pray for our family members. God's Word states those that love Jerusalem will prosper (Psalms 122:6). Notice that Psalms 122:9 says, *"because of the house of the LORD our God I will seek thy good"*. Many of us have never been taught to pray for Israel and bless them. God's promise that a blessing would come upon those who would bless Israel still holds true. When we truly understand the heart of God and our Jewish heritage, we will not fail to bless them daily.

Give Us This Day Our Daily Bread. And Forgive Us Our Debts, As We Forgive Our Debtors.
(Matt 6:11-12)

As king-priests, we stand in the gap and repent for all men. As we thank God for Jesus the "Bread of Life", we are thanking Him for His daily provision to do battle, overcome and be delivered. When we spiritually partake of communion and have fellowship with the Lord, we receive His full power. This prepares us to enter into spiritual warfare and intercede for all men.

Prayer:
5. *The Table Of Shewbread*

FATHER I STAND IN THE GAP AND REPENT FOR ALL. THANK YOU THAT JESUS IS THE BREAD OF LIFE AND MY POWER TO DO BATTLE. I SPIRITUALLY PARTAKE OF COMMUNION, PUT ON YOUR ARMOR AND INTERCEDE FIRST FOR YOUR PURPOSES AND THEN PRAY MY OWN PETITIONS.
[Give Us This Day Our Daily Bread. And Forgive Us Our Debts, As We Forgive Our Debtors]

Father as I come to Your Table as a king-priest and intercessor, I stand in the gap for the Jews, the entire Body of Christ, the unsaved, and for the leaders of this world **(Ezek 22:30)**. I stand in the gap and repent for we have all sinned, transgressed Your laws, committed iniquity, shed innocent blood, operated in unforgiveness, and have done wickedly in Your sight. **I John 1:9,** says if we confess our sins, You are faithful and just to forgive us. Father, forgive and cleanse us with the Blood of Jesus. Father, as we spiritually partake of communion, the broken body and shed Blood of Jesus, we thank You that Jesus is the "Bread of Life". His body and Blood is our nourishment, strength and power to be victorious over all works of the enemy. It is also the "Children's Bread of Deliverance", therefore we are delivered from every foe within and without. We put on the whole of armor of God according to **Eph 6:10-20.** We are strong in the Lord and in the power of His might. The weapons of our warfare are not carnal but they are mighty through God for the pulling down of strongholds **(II Cor 10: 4-5).** You have given us authority to tread upon serpents and scorpions, and over all of the power of the enemy and nothing shall by any means hurt us **(Luke 10:19).** We bind every strong man that is set against us and loose the Angel of the Lord to plunder their house and spoil their goods **(Matt 12:29).** According to **II Tim 4:18,** Father we declare that You will deliver us from every evil work and preserve us for Your heavenly kingdom. We pray that the unsaved will come to know Jesus Christ as Lord and Savior **(Ps 2:8).** We ask for the heathen nations as our inheritance and the uttermost parts of the earth as our possession. We also pray for the fear of God to fall upon every leader all over the world, thereby bringing them to repentance. We declare that Your people will lead a quiet and peaceable life in all godliness and honesty and the gospel of Jesus Christ will continue to spread unhindered all over the world **(I Tim 2:2).** Father we ask that we receive the spirit of wisdom and revelation in the knowledge of You, that the eyes of our understanding are enlightened that we might know the hope of our calling and to know the surpassing fullness of Your love **(Eph 1:17-23 -- 3:14-21).** We pray for the peace of Jerusalem, peace within their walls and prosperity within their palaces and we seek their highest good **(Ps 122:6-9).** We pray that the Body of Christ will come into the unity of faith, unto the knowledge of the Son of God, unto a perfect man, to the measure of the stature of the fullness of Christ **(Eph 4:13).**

The Altar Of Incense

Ex 30:1-3
And thou shalt make an altar to burn incense upon: of shittim wood shalt thou make it. A cubit shall be the length thereof, and a cubit the breadth thereof; foursquare shall it be: and two cubits shall be the height thereof: the horns thereof shall be of the same. And thou shalt overlay it with pure gold, the top thereof, and the sides thereof round about, and the horns thereof; and thou shalt make unto it a crown of gold round about.

The Altar of Incense is the perfect shadow to the fulfillment of true worship. Worship is our highest calling and the purpose for which we were created. On this earth, we are in preparation for the *"timeless"* ministry of giving worship unto the Lord. In John 4:23, Jesus tells us the Father is looking for *"true worshippers"*, those who will worship Him in spirit and in truth. This Altar was anointed with blood and oil, and a unique blend of spices was burned as incense on this Altar. The anointing oil symbolized worshipping the Lord in *"spirit"* and the incense symbolized worshipping Him in *"truth"*. In order to produce true worship these ingredients must be present. Additionally hot coals, used to burn the sacrifice, were taken from the Brazen Altar to burn the incense. Our worship will not rise without the hot coals of our committed life in a covenant relationship with God.

Anointing Oil

The anointing oil had five main ingredients, which were MYRRH, CINNAMON, CALAMUS, CASSIA and OLIVE OIL (Exodus 30:22-25). As discussed earlier, in the Priesthood chapter, these ingredients symbolize five graces of the Holy

Spirit that will transform us into true worshippers. The anointing oil was symbolic of the Holy Spirit and His nature. In order to worship the Lord in spirit, we must possess the nature and character of the Holy Spirit. The fruit of the Spirit, found in Galatians 5:22-23, reflect the nature of the Holy Spirit. However, it should also reflect the fruit of the recreated human spirit. Our fruit can only be developed or ripened by spending time in the presence of God.

As we come to the realization that we are *"love"* creatures, born of a *"LOVE"* God, we will determine to walk in the agape love of God. First Corinthians 13 states love is the greatest fruit and it will abide throughout eternity. We need to apply to our lives these five ingredients or graces found in the anointing oil. This will cause us to walk in such love and power that we are able to produce the fruit of true worshippers. God will be able to come into His garden, the Church, and eat of our pleasant fruit (Song of Solomon 4:16).

Worship Incense

Worshipping the Lord in truth involves our heart attitudes or motivations. In Exodus 30:34, the five ingredients in the incense were stacte, onycha, galbanum, frankincense and salt. They represent heart motivations that are pleasing to the Lord. A characteristic of STACTE, which is the purest myrrh, is that it is free flowing. The true worshipper is spontaneous and free flowing in his relationship with God. ONYCHA comes from an aromatic deep-sea fish. As true worshippers, when we feed upon the Word of God, we become a sweet smelling fragrance unto the Lord. We should also go deep with the Lord, and come to Him with an open, honest, and transparent heart.

GALBANUM is a bitter gum used as a medicine and is symbolic of God healing our broken heart. We can bring our broken hearts and dreams and present them to the Lord as an attitude of worship. He will mend our hearts and fulfill greater dreams than we thought possible. FRANKINCENSE is a sweet smelling gum that is symbolic of Jesus. It speaks to us of purity, prayer, intercession, and righteousness. SALT, a sign of covenant, was added to temper the mixture. Salt is symbolic of speech that is pure and full of grace (Colossians 4:6).

In summary, God says come to Him with spontaneity, transparency, depth, and humility. We take these ingredients and mix them with the purity of Jesus blended with salt, which is seasoned covenant speech, to create true worship incense. When we worship God with the *"graces"* and *"heart attitudes"* which are symbolized by the anointing oil and worship incense, our lives begin to conform to the plan and purpose of God!

The Apostle and High Priest

According to Hebrews 7:25, the perpetual ministry of Jesus is to make intercession for us, as our High Priest. He entered into the presence of God for us on the basis of His finished work on Calvary. He perfects our petitions, prayers and worship and presents them to the Father. According to Hebrews 3:1, He is the *"Apostle and High Priest of our profession"* or confession. And He is anointed to bring every word to pass that we speak, as it lines up with the Word of God.

And Lead Us Not Into Temptation, But Deliver Us From Evil.
(Matt 6:13)

When we ask God to purge our hearts and perfect His love within us, we are asking for deliverance from the evil one. Demonic forces cannot stand against the agape love of God. Therefore, we are to walk in love, as directed by I Corinthians 13, and keep a repentant heart. It is important that we ask the Holy Spirit to come into our hearts and purge us daily. We are then assured of having a pure heart before God.

Prayer:
6. *The Altar Of Incense*

FATHER CLEANSE MY HEART AND PERFECT YOUR LOVE AND THE FRUIT OF THE SPIRIT WITHIN ME.
[And Lead Us Not Into Temptation, But Deliver Us From Evil]

Father create in me a clean heart, O God; and renew a right spirit within me **(Ps 51:10).** Perfect Your love in my life according to **I Cor 13.** I want the fruit of the Spirit to ripen in me **(Gal 5:22-23 - II Peter 1:5-8).** I pray for love, joy, peace, longsuffering, gentleness, goodness, faith, meekness and temperance: balanced with the gifts of the Spirit **(I Cor 12:8-10).** Father God, I bring You worship attitudes of spontaneity, openness, honesty, transparency, brokenness, the sweet fragrance of Jesus, and covenant speech. I ask You to come into my heart, and let the light of Your countenance purge away all that is not pleasing to You and deliver me from evil **(Ps 4:6).** I bring to You my weaknesses, hurts, wounds, broken dreams and broken heart. I cast all of my cares upon You for You care for me **(I Peter 5:7).** **Heb 7:25** says that Jesus is able to deliver me and ever lives to make intercession for me. Jesus is the Apostle and High Priest of my profession and confession **(Heb 3:1).** I thank You Lord Jesus for perfecting my prayers, worship, and all that concerns me **(Ps 138:8).** I also ask You to take the coal and cleanse my lips, for life and death are in the power of the tongue **(Prov 18:21).** Put a guard over my mouth so that I will say only Your words of peace and prosperity over myself and others **(Col 4:6).** Father I thank You that I have a covenant relationship with You. I am blessed of God Most High, the possessor of heaven and earth and blessed be God Most High; that has delivered all of my enemies into my hand **(Gen 14:19-20).**

The Veil Of The Secret Place

Ex 26:31
And thou shalt make a vail of blue, and purple, and scarlet, and fine twined linen of cunning work: with cherubims shall it be made:

The veil of the Secret Place was made of fine linen, interwoven with three cherubim. The cherubim symbolized the fullness of the Godhead. The veil divided the Holy Place from the Holy of Holies, and guarded the entrance to the presence of God. The veil was positioned behind the Altar of Incense. The priests, in their daily ministry, would place incense upon the Altar and the cloud of fragrant perfume would permeate the veil and go into the presence of God. But only the High Priest could enter beyond the veil, and only on the Day of Atonement. The earthly ministry of Jesus relates to the Outer and Inner Courts, while His heavenly ministry relates to the Secret Place.

After the death of Jesus, He entered into His heavenly ministry, as High Priest of the House of God (Hebrews 8:1-2). Matthew 27:51 tells us that the veil of the Temple was torn in two from *"TOP"* to bottom at the death of Jesus. Hebrews 10:20 tells us that Jesus consecrated a *"new and living"* way into the presence of God for us through the *"veil"* of His flesh. As our High Priest, He purges our heart and conscience and draws us near to Him (Hebrews 10:22). At this point we shed the *"veil"* of our flesh, in prayer, and our spirits soar into God's presence. This is the only way for our spirits to experience complete satisfaction in this life. It is joy unspeakable and full of glory!

The Ark Of The Covenant

Ex 25:17-21
And thou shalt make a mercy seat of pure gold: two cubits and a half shall be the length thereof, and a cubit and a half the breadth thereof. And thou shalt make two cherubims of gold, of beaten work shalt thou make them, in the two ends of the mercy seat. And make one cherub on the one end, and the other cherub on the other end: even of the mercy seat shall ye make the cherubims on the two ends thereof. And the cherubims shall stretch forth their wings on high, covering the mercy seat with their wings, and their faces shall look one to another; toward the mercy seat shall the faces of the cherubims be. And thou shalt put the mercy seat above upon the ark; and in the ark thou shalt put the testimony that I shall give thee.

The Ark of the Covenant was a chest overlaid with gold within and without (Exodus 25:10-11). The cover was called the Mercy Seat, and it means, *"to atone"* or *"cover"*. This was where the blood of the sacrifice was placed on the Day of Atonement. There were Cherubim on each end of the Mercy Seat and the faces of the Cherubim looked toward one another and towards the Mercy Seat. This symbolized the Father, Son, and Holy Spirit in the work of redemption. The Mercy Seat is our Lord Jesus Christ and the Cherubim are the Father and Holy Spirit looking with favor upon the Blood sacrifice of the Son. Jesus kept the Law, and was obedient to God with all His heart, soul, mind, and strength. His complete compliance to the Law is credited to our account. Now when the Father looks at us, He sees us through the Blood of Jesus, thereby viewing us as perfect!!!

The Day Of Atonement

Once a year, on the Day of Atonement, the high priest entered the Most Holy Place with blood, sprinkled it once on the Mercy Seat and seven times before it on the ground (Leviticus 16:14). Seven is the number of perfection and fullness. The Blood of Jesus is the sum total of perfection and the fulfillment of this type and shadow. It is only the Blood of Jesus that has the power to restore all things to proper order!

Once we enter God's presence, we realize that there are still things within us that do not measure up to His standards of holiness. The only way we can stand in the light of His glory and presence is because His Blood is there on the Mercy Seat, speaking on our behalf. The Father and Holy Spirit (Cherubim) look upon the Blood of Jesus and us with contentment.

According to Exodus 25:22, the Lord would meet and commune with the High Priest from above the Mercy Seat between the two Cherubim. Numbers 7:89 states the voice of the Lord came from the Mercy Seat where the blood was applied. Thank God the Blood of Jesus was applied to the heavenly Mercy Seat and it is always there speaking FOR US and TO US! As the Lord meets with and communes with us in the Secret Place, we get clear and distinct direction concerning our destiny in Him. Too often, we have failed to come into His presence so we can hear His voice. The Lord may not be inclined to shout to the Outer or Inner Courts, His will and purpose for our lives.

Jesus Was The Ark
The Carrier Of God's Presence

Jesus was the carrier of God's presence on the earth. In Colossians 2:9, we are told in Him, dwelt the fullness of the Godhead (Father, Son, and Holy Spirit) bodily. We know it was God in Christ reconciling the world unto Himself. But now we have entered into the realm where the God in Christ has become the Christ in us, and as Colossians 1:27 tells us, it is Christ in us; the hope of glory! We are the treasure chests of the Lord and He has deposited the treasure of the Holy Spirit inside of us. The *"excellency of the power"* is of God and not of man (II Corinthians 4:7).

Contents Of The Ark

According to Hebrews 9:4 the contents of the Ark were as follows:

The Golden Pot Of Manna

The Ark housed the Golden Pot of Manna. It was a reminder of how God supernaturally fed the Israelites in the wilderness with Manna from heaven. It is also a reminder of the *"Hidden Manna"* or *"Bread from Heaven"* that Melchizedek gave to Abraham to cut covenant. This was God's promise that Jesus would be within us to give us the strength of the Almighty for provision, power and deliverance. According to Revelation 2:17, there is hidden Manna that is available to him that overcomes. We must overcome the world, the flesh, and the devil to enter into our covenant relationship to be king-priests unto God.

Aaron's Rod

Aaron's Rod that blossomed was also in the Ark. It brought forth buds, blossoms, and almonds (Numbers 17:8). Almonds are symbolic of resurrection power and awakening. As king-priests we are to bud, blossom, and bring forth fruit with the resurrection power of our Lord. By praying according to Pattern, we will transform our lives and the lives of every precious stone in our breastplate.

The Tables Of The Law

The third item in the Ark was the Tables of the Law, the Ten Commandments, which were given to Moses on Mount Sinai. Under the New Covenant, God promised to write His laws in our minds and our hearts. As king-priests, we are to know and declare the Word of God according to Pattern so all will come to know Him (Hebrews 8:10-11).

Christ Entered Heaven Itself

Hebrews 9:24 states that Christ appeared in heaven in the presence of God for us. After the resurrection of Jesus, He entered the heavenly sanctuary with His Blood and placed it on the Mercy Seat. His Blood is speaking now and forever throughout the endless ages of eternity. It is speaking of His mercies and His wonderful plan of redemption!

Pleasures Forevermore!

We can forever dwell beneath the shadow of His wings in this Secret Place. Psalms 16:11 states: *"Thou wilt shew me the path of life: in thy presence is fulness of joy; at thy right hand there are pleasures for evermore"*. The *"path of life"* is the journey through the Tabernacle into the very presence of God. There is no greater joy in life than to be in the King's presence!

For Thine Is The Kingdom, And The Power, And The Glory, For Ever. Amen. (Matt 6:13)

We come into the Most Holy Place, to exalt the Father, Son, and Holy Spirit. The Lord Jesus brought the Kingdom of God to the earth. The Holy Spirit brought the power of God to every believer and the Father will bring the glory that will cover the earth as the waters cover the sea. When we declare God's total dominion and supremacy, we establish it in our lives and upon the earth.

Prayer:
7. *The Ark Of The Covenant*

FATHER THANK YOU FOR LETTING ME COME INTO YOUR HOLY PRESENCE.

[For Thine Is The Kingdom, And The Power, And The Glory, For Ever. A-Men.]

You have shown me the path of life: in Your presence is fullness of joy; at Your right hand there are pleasures for evermore **(Ps 16:11).** Daddy thank You for the precious Blood of Jesus that is speaking from the Mercy Seat, proclaiming greater things than that of Abel **(Heb 12:24).** I am so grateful Daddy, that when You look at me, You do not see me, but You see Jesus. Daddy God, thank You for making me a vessel that is filled with Your presence **(Col 1:27).** Your Laws are written upon my heart and in my mind **(Heb 8:10)**. I speak and declare the truth of Your Word. I have revelation knowledge, and bud, blossom and bring forth fruit in resurrection power. The fruit and the gifts of the Spirit are operating in my life in perfect balance. I am like the Ark, a golden vessel, filled with Your covenant promises and with Your glory **(Isa 60:1-3).** I worship You Daddy as the Giver and the Source of all life. I worship You Holy Spirit and I thank You for being the lover of my soul, my Comforter and my closest friend. I worship You Lord Jesus, for You are the King of Glory, the Lord of Hosts, Captain of heaven's armies, and the Lord strong and mighty **(Ps 24:7).** I declare that Jesus is Lord, and His dominion is everlasting. For thine is the kingdom, the power and the glory for ever and ever, Amen.

The Tabernacle
Prayer Pattern Illustration

ARK OF THE COVENANT
Jesus the Carrier
of the Presence of God

7. THE HOLY OF HOLIES - THE PRESENCE OF GOD
For Thine Is The Kingdom, And The Power,
And The Glory, For Ever. A-Men.

THE ALTAR OF INCENSE
Jesus the Apostle
and High Priest

6. PURGE YOUR HEART AND WORSHIP
HIM IN SPIRIT AND IN TRUTH
And Lead Us Not Into Temptation,
But Deliver Us From Evil

THE LAMPSTAND
Jesus the Light
of the World

TABLE OF SHEWBREAD
Jesus the Bread
of the Life

4. THANK GOD FOR THE ANOINTING
OF THE HOLY GHOST
In Earth, As It Is In Heaven

5. STAND IN THE GAP, REPENT AND
INTERCEDE FOR ALL MEN
Give Us This Day Our Daily Bread. And Forgive
Us Our Debts, As We Forgive Our Debtors

BRAZEN LAVER
Jesus the Word
of God made flesh

3. THANK GOD FOR HIS WORD
Thy Will Be Done

BRAZEN ALTAR
Jesus the sinless Lamb
became the Eternal Sacrifice

2. THANK GOD FOR THE BLOOD OF JESUS CHRIST
Thy Kingdom Come

1. REPENT AND ENTER HIS GATES WITH THANKSGIVING
Our Father Which Art In Heaven, Hallowed Be Thy Name

The Tabernacle Prayer

YOUR KING-PRIEST MINISTRY

Revelation 1:5-6 states the Blood of Jesus has made us kings and priests unto God. As kings we are to declare and decree the Word of God. As priests we are to become true worshippers and intercessors praying for the perfection of the Saints and the salvation of lost souls. Therefore, as you pray keep in mind you are a king-priest fulfilling the Word of God. You have been anointed and appointed to stand in the gap and intercede for the world.

This prayer is constructed in the order of the Tabernacle of Moses. It is also in the order of the Lord's Prayer in **Matthew 6:9-13.** Before you begin any prayer you need to repent. **Psalms 66:18** states, that if you regard iniquity in your heart, the Lord will not hear you. Therefore it is appropriate that you take care of your sin by repenting. This prayer is designed to be short and can be read in approximately fifteen minutes. However, you can take your time by praying the Word and then praying in tongues. We recommend that you pray this prayer each morning and/or record it on tape so you can play it and pray along. It is necessary that you fill up your spirit with prayer daily. This Prayer Pattern is unlimited, so feel free to find your own scriptures. Talk to God in your own words; just make sure that you use one or more scriptures for each section. Remember God's Word will not return unto Him void, so use His Word to make your prayers more powerful.

¹ *The Gate - Repentance*

FATHER WE REPENT AND CONFESS OUR SINS.

Father, have mercy upon us according to Your loving kindness and tender mercies and blot out our transgressions. Wash us from iniquity and cleanse us from sin. For against You and You only we have sinned **(Ps 51:1-4).** Father in the name of Jesus, we repent for every sin, known, unknown, omitted, and committed. We repent for unforgiveness and we release and forgive all **(Mark 11:25).** We ask You to cleanse us from secret faults and keep us back from presumptuous sins; and let them not have dominion over us: then we shall be upright, and innocent from the great transgression **(Ps 19:12-13).** Father, we thank You that Your Word says in **I John 1:9,** If we confess our sins, You are faithful and just to forgive us, and to cleanse us from all unrighteousness. Create in us a clean heart and renew a right spirit within us and let the words of our mouth and the meditation of our heart be acceptable in Your sight O Lord our strength and Redeemer **(Ps 51:10) -- (Ps 19:14).**

The Gate - Thanksgiving

FATHER WE ENTER YOUR GATES WITH THANKSGIVING.
[Our Father Which Art In Heaven, Hallowed Be Thy Name]

Father we praise You, hallow Your holy name, and thank You for Your love. Lord we praise You for Your mighty acts and we praise You according to Your excellent greatness **(Ps 150:1-2).** O Lord, our Lord how excellent is Your name in all the earth **(Ps 8:1)!** The name of the Lord is a strong tower and the righteous run into it and are safe **(Prov 18:10).** O magnify the Lord with us, and let's exalt His name together **(Ps 34:3).** The Lord's name is to be praised from the rising of the sun to the going down of the same **(Ps 113:3).** Every day we will bless You Lord, and we will praise Your name forever and ever **(Ps 145:2).**

(Continue to bless the lord and give thanks for all that He has done for you.)

2 *The Brazen Altar*

FATHER, THANK YOU FOR THE BLOOD OF JESUS CHRIST.
[Thy Kingdom Come]

Father, thank You for loving us so much that You gave Your only begotten Son, that whosoever shall believe in Him should not perish but have everlasting life **(John 3:16).** He was wounded for our transgressions, He was bruised for our iniquities: the chastisement of our peace was upon Him; and with His stripes we are healed **(Isa 53:5).** Thank You Lord Jesus for blotting out the handwriting of the ordinances that were against us and taking them out of the way by nailing them to Your cross. In the process You defeated and triumphed over every evil power and made a show of them openly **(Col 2:14-15).** Father God, we thank You for the precious Blood of Jesus that was shed for the remission of all our sins. We plead and apply the Blood of Jesus to every part of our lives and every precious stone in our breastplate.

Gal 3:13 assures us that Christ has redeemed us from every curse over our lives, that we may partake of the blessings of Abraham. Thank You Lord Jesus for redeeming us by Your Blood and making us king-priests unto God to reign on this earth **(Rev 5:9-10)**. Father we thank You that Your kingdom has come in our lives.

3 *The Brazen Laver*

FATHER THANK YOU FOR YOUR WORD.
[Thy Will Be Done]

Father, we thank You that **John 1:1** says, in the beginning was the Word, and the Word was with God, and the Word was God. **John 1:14** says that the Word was made flesh, and dwelt among us, (and we beheld His glory, the glory of the only begotten of the Father), full of grace and truth. Jesus is the Word made flesh. Your Word is made flesh or manifested in our lives, as we establish Your Word upon this earth. Your Word is health and healing to all of our flesh **(Prov 4:22)**. Your Word is quick and powerful and sharper than any two-edged sword and is able to divide the soul and spirit, the joints and marrow, and discern the thoughts and intents of the heart **(Heb 4:12)**. Your Word is a lamp unto our feet, and a light unto our path **(Ps 119:105)**. We receive the blessings of **Deut 28:1-14**, because we hearken diligently unto Your Word. We thank You Father that we have been sanctified and cleansed with the washing of water by the Word of God **(Eph 5:26)**. Your Word is Your will, therefore let Your will be done in our lives.

(This is where you can add specific "Word" declarations concerning personal and corporate prayer objectives)

4 *The Golden Candlestick*

FATHER THANK YOU FOR THE ANOINTING OF THE HOLY SPIRIT.
[In Earth, As It Is In Heaven]

In **John 8:12** Jesus said, I am the Light of the world and he that follows Me shall not walk in darkness but shall have the light of life. Father thank You for the light of life, which is the anointing. Jesus is the "Light of the world" and He has caused us to be a reflector of that light, which will bring glory to our Heavenly Father **(Matt 5:14-16)**. **Acts 10:38** states, that God anointed Jesus of Nazareth with the Holy Ghost and with power: who went about doing good, and healing all that were oppressed of the devil; for God was with Him. We are also anointed with the Holy Spirit and we are born of God for the purpose of destroying the works of darkness **(I John 3:8)**. Jesus said in **John 14:12,** he that believes on Me, the works that I do he shall do also and greater works than these. Thank You Lord for the anointing of the Holy Spirit and the gifts of the Spirit to do these greater works. We ask You, Holy Spirit, to flow through us as You purpose with Your gifts, the gift of faith, gifts of healing, working of miracles, word of wisdom, word of knowledge, discerning of spirits, tongues, interpretation of tongues, and prophecy **(I Cor 12:8-10)**. We have the sevenfold anointing; the Spirit of the Lord, the spirit of wisdom and understanding, the spirit of counsel and might, the spirit of knowledge, and of the fear of the Lord **(Isa 11:2)**.

Father, correct us, so that nothing will hinder Your power from flowing through us and we can bring forth pure and holy light. Father, we thank You for the Holy Spirit, Who brings forth Your power from heaven. We also thank You for allowing us to share Your light all over this world.

5 The Table Of Shewbread

FATHER WE STAND IN THE GAP AND REPENT FOR ALL. THANK YOU THAT JESUS IS THE BREAD OF LIFE AND OUR POWER TO DO BATTLE. WE SPIRITUALLY PARTAKE OF COMMUNION, PUT ON YOUR ARMOR AND INTERCEDE FIRST FOR YOUR PURPOSES AND THEN PRAY OUR OWN PETITIONS. *[Give Us This Day Our Daily Bread. And Forgive Us Our Debts, As We Forgive Our Debtors]*

Father as we come to Your Table as king-priests and intercessors, we stand in the gap for the Jews, the entire Body of Christ, the unsaved, and for the leaders of this world **(Ezek 22:30)**. We stand in the gap and repent for we have all sinned, transgressed Your laws, committed iniquity, shed innocent blood, operated in unforgiveness, and have done wickedly in Your sight. **I John 1:9** says, if we confess our sins, You are faithful and just to forgive us. Father forgive and cleanse us with the Blood of Jesus. Father, as we spiritually partake of communion, the broken body and shed Blood of Jesus, we thank You that Jesus is the "Bread of Life". His body and Blood is our nourishment, strength and power to be victorious over all works of the enemy. It is also the "Children's Bread of Deliverance", therefore we are delivered from every foe within and without. We put on the whole of armor of God according to **Eph 6:10-20.** We are strong in the Lord and in the power of His might. The weapons of our warfare are not carnal but they are mighty through God for the pulling down of strongholds **(II Cor 10: 4-5).** You have given us authority to tread upon serpents and scorpions, and over all of the power of the enemy and nothing shall by any means hurt us **(Luke 10:19).** We bind every strong man that is set against us and loose the Angel of the Lord to plunder their house and spoil their goods **(Matt 12:29).** According to **II Tim 4:18,** Father we declare that You will deliver us from every evil work and preserve us for Your heavenly kingdom. We pray that the unsaved will come to know Jesus Christ as Lord and Savior **(Ps 2:8).** We ask for the heathen nations as our inheritance and the uttermost parts of the earth as our possession. We also pray for the fear of God to fall upon every leader all over the world, thereby bringing them to repentance. We declare that Your people will lead a quiet and peaceable life in all godliness and honesty and the gospel of Jesus Christ will continue to spread unhindered all over the world **(I Tim 2:2).** Father we ask that we receive the spirit of wisdom and revelation in the knowledge of You, that the eyes of our understanding are enlightened that we might know the hope of our calling and to know the surpassing fullness of Your love **(Eph 1:17-23 -- 3:14-21).** We pray for the peace of Jerusalem, peace within their walls and prosperity within their palaces and we seek their highest good **(Ps 122:6-9)**. We pray that the Body of Christ will come into the unity of faith, unto the knowledge of the Son of God, unto a perfect man, to the measure of the stature of the fullness of Christ **(Eph 4:13)**.

(You can now pray your own petitions)

6 *The Altar Of Incense*

FATHER CLEANSE OUR HEARTS AND PERFECT YOUR LOVE AND THE FRUIT OF THE SPIRIT WITHIN US.
[And Lead Us Not Into Temptation, But Deliver Us From Evil]

Father create in us a clean heart, O God; and renew a right spirit within us **(Ps 51:10)**. Perfect Your love in our lives according to **I Cor 13**. We want the fruit of the Spirit to ripen in us **(Gal 5:22-23 - II Peter 1:5-8)**. We pray for love, joy, peace, longsuffering, gentleness, goodness, faith, meekness and temperance: balanced with the gifts of the Spirit **(I Cor 12:8-10)**. Father God, we bring You worship attitudes of spontaneity, honesty, transparency, brokenness, the sweet fragrance of Jesus, and covenant speech. We ask You to come into our hearts, and let the light of Your countenance purge away all that is not pleasing to You and deliver us from evil **(Ps 4:6)**. We bring to You our weaknesses, hurts, wounds, broken dreams and broken hearts. We cast all of our cares upon You for You care for us **(I Peter 5:7)**. **Heb 7:25** says that Jesus is able to deliver us and ever lives to make intercession for us. Jesus is the Apostle and High Priest of our profession and confession **(Heb 3:1)**. We thank You Lord Jesus for perfecting our prayers, worship, and all that concerns us **(Ps 138:8)**. We also ask You to take the coal and cleanse our lips, for life and death are in the power of the tongue **(Prov 18:21)**. Put a guard over our mouths so that we will say only Your words of peace and prosperity over ourselves and others **(Col 4:6)**. Father we thank You that we have a covenant relationship with You. We are blessed of God Most High, the possessor of heaven and earth and blessed be God Most High; that has delivered all of our enemies into our hand **(Gen 14:19-20)**.

7 *The Ark Of The Covenant*

FATHER THANK YOU FOR LETTING US COME INTO YOUR HOLY PRESENCE. *[For Thine Is The Kingdom, And The Power, And The Glory, For Ever. A-Men.]*

You have shown us the path of life: in Your presence is fullness of joy; at Your right hand there are pleasures for evermore **(Ps 16:11)**. Daddy thank You for the precious Blood of Jesus that is speaking from the Mercy Seat, proclaiming greater things than that of Abel **(Heb 12:24)**. We are so grateful Daddy, that when You look at us, You do not see us, but You see Jesus. Daddy God, thank You for making us vessels that are filled with Your presence **(Col 1:27)**. Your Laws are

written upon our hearts and in our minds **(Heb 8:10).**
We speak and declare the truth of Your Word. We have
revelation knowledge, and bud, blossom and bring forth
fruit in resurrection power. The fruit and the gifts of
the Spirit are operating in our lives in perfect balance.
We are like the Ark, golden vessels, filled with Your
covenant promises and with Your glory **(Isa 60:1-3).**
We worship You, Daddy, as the Giver and the Source of
all life. We worship You, Holy Spirit, and we thank You
for being the lover of our souls, our Comforter and our
closest friend. We worship You, Lord Jesus, for You are
the King of Glory, the Lord of Hosts, Captain of
heaven's armies, and the Lord strong and mighty **(Ps
24:7).** We declare that Jesus is Lord, and His dominion
is everlasting. For thine is the kingdom, the power and
the glory for ever and ever, Amen.

*Then begin to worship the entire Godhead with the
fruit of your lips, and with a "new song" in tongues
or your understanding (I Cor 14:15). The Lord
may also have you read scripture to Him.
The Psalms and/or Revelation 5
are always great.*

**FOLLOW THE HOLY SPIRIT AND
WE GUARANTEE YOU, YOUR
LIFE WILL NEVER BE
THE SAME!!!**

**WE OVERCOME BY THE BLOOD
OF THE LAMB AND THE WORD
OF OUR TESTIMONY!!!
(Rev 12:11)**

Short Tabernacle Prayer

Father we come to You in the name of Jesus, repenting of all of our sins. We repent for sins known and unknown, sins of word, thought and deed, and also secret faults **(Ps 51:1-4)**. Cleanse us according to **I John 1:9;** Your Word states if we confess our sins, You are faithful and just to forgive us and cleanse us from all unrighteousness. Father we enter Your gates with thanksgiving and Your courts with praise, exalting the name of Jesus which is above every name **(Eph 1:20-21)**. We declare that Jesus is Lord over this day.

Father we thank You that Jesus is the Lamb of God, Who shed His Blood for our sins and complete deliverance **(John 1:29 - John 3:16)**.

Father, we also thank You that Jesus is the Word made flesh **(John 1:14)** and You sent Your Word to heal us and deliver us from our destructions **(Ps 107:20)**. We also thank You for washing us by the water of Your Word so we can come forth as Your bride, holy and pure **(Eph 5:26-27)**.

We exalt You Father for the power and the anointing of the Holy Spirit, making us Your Lampstand **(Matt 5:14-16)**. We reflect Your light and walk in miracles, signs, and wonders.

Father we come to stand in the gap and repent for all mankind. We have all sinned and fallen short of Your glory and we ask for Your forgiveness **(Dan 9:5, 19)**. As we spiritually receive communion, the broken body and shed Blood of Jesus, we gain full power to war, battle and overcome. We put on the whole armor of God and pray for every precious stone in our breastplate, the Lost, the Leadership, the Body of Christ and the Jewish Nation **(I Tim 2:1-4)**. We declare that the Lord will deliver us from every evil work and preserve us for His heavenly kingdom – to Him be the glory for ever and ever **(II Tim 4:18)**. We pray for the peace of Jerusalem, peace within their walls, and prosperity within their palaces **(Ps 122:6-9)**. Father we thank You for the blessing over our lives that You promised us for praying for Israel **(Gen 12:3)**. We thank You that we all come into the unity of faith perfected in Christ **(Eph 4:13)**.

We come to You as true worshippers in the earth, worshipping You in spirit and in truth **(John 4:23-24)**. We purge our hearts and bring that perfect blend of heart motivations and attitudes **(Gal 5:22-23)**. We exalt Jesus the Apostle and High Priest of the House of God. He makes this prayer and our worship perfect before You and leads us into Your presence **(Heb 3:1)**.

Father we come beyond the Veil into Your presence, worshipping at the Mercy Seat, Your throne of grace **(Heb 4:16)**. We worship You Father, Jesus the Lamb of God, and Holy Spirit in the joy of Your presence **(Ps 16:11)**. We exalt You, Father, and magnify Your name and the name of Jesus in all the earth. We love You and we thank You for loving us! For thine is the kingdom, the power and the glory forever! Amen **(Matt 6:13)**.

Model For Creating Your Own Prayer

1. **Repent**
   (Father We Repent And Confess Our Sins)

   _____

   _____

   _____

   Enter His Gates With Thanksgiving
   [Our Father Which Art In Heaven, Hallowed Be Thy Name]

   _____

   _____

   _____

2. **Thank God For The Blood Of Jesus Christ**
   [Thy Kingdom Come]

   _____

   _____

   _____

3. **Thank God For His Word**
   [Thy Will Be Done]

   _____

   _____

   _____

4. **Thank God For The Anointing Of The Holy Spirit**
   [In Earth, As It Is In Heaven]

   _____

   _____

   _____

5. **Stand In The Gap, Repent, And Intercede For The World**
   [Give Us This Day Our Daily Bread. And Forgive Us Our Debts, As We Forgive Our Debtors]

   _____

   _____

   _____

6. **Purge Your Heart And Worship God In Spirit And In Truth**
   [And Lead Us Not Into Temptation, But Deliver Us From Evil]

   _____

   _____

   _____

7. **Worship The Father, Son And Holy Spirit**
   [For Thine Is The Kingdom, And The Power, And The Glory, For Ever. A-Men.]

   _____

   _____

   _____

Chapter Twelve

Jerusalem

In 1996, the 3,000-year celebration of Jerusalem was taking place. One day while in prayer, we received Isaiah 56:7. It states; *"Even them will I bring to my holy mountain, and make them joyful in my house of prayer: their burnt offerings and their sacrifices shall be accepted upon mine altar; for mine house shall be called an house of prayer for all people"*. Then God placed a strong desire within us to go to Jerusalem. During this historic year, in October 1996, we went to the Holy Land. We knew that this was to be a prayer journey to pray the Tabernacle Prayer and worship in Jerusalem.

During our flight to Jerusalem there was a three-hour layover in West Germany. We began to pray the Tabernacle Prayer in the airport and we were totally surprised, as the Holy Spirit began to lead us in an awesome prayer of repentance for the sins of Germany against the Jewish nation. He also led us in a prayer of repentance for the Jewish nation's sin of unforgiveness towards Germany! By beginning with repentance, which is always necessary before blessing, we began to see the divine order and government of God in this prayer journey.

The first night in Jerusalem, after falling asleep, I was awakened by the Lord. He told me over and over emphatically that we had to repent for the sin of idolatry. Each place we visited we repented and prayed according to Pattern. Most notably, at the Wailing Wall, (the Western Wall of the last Temple), we repented for all sins and applied the Blood of Jesus over the entire area. According to Pattern, we brought all of God's people together as one and worshipped there before Him. The power of God was incredibly strong! It was as if all of heaven was waiting for this type of prayer!

At the Garden of Gethsemane we also repented, prayed, and worshipped according to Pattern. At the end of the prayer, as we were calling forth the precious fruit of the earth (James 5:7), immediately the Church bells rang twelve times! The number twelve represents apostolic government and fullness. It was as if God was confirming His Word and the beginning of apostolic fullness that would bring restoration and revival!

We began to understand more of the significance of these events as they pertained to the 3,000-year celebration. King David had established Jerusalem as a city 3,000 years ago. He was the first one to combine the offices of king and priest. We believe that the timing of our trip was a divine appointment, to call forth the New Testament king-priests, who would pray and worship according to God's divine pattern. When the king-priests come forth in power, the knowledge of the glory of the Lord will cover the earth as the waters cover the sea!

Hab 2:14
For the earth shall be filled with the knowledge of the glory of the LORD, as the waters cover the sea.

Pray With Us!

Ps 87
His foundation is in the holy mountains. The LORD loveth the gates of Zion more than all the dwellings of Jacob. Glorious things are spoken of thee, O city of God. Selah. I will make mention of Rahab and Babylon to them that know me: behold Philistia, and Tyre, with Ethiopia; this man was born there. And of Zion it shall be said, This and that man was born in her: and the highest himself shall establish her. THE LORD SHALL COUNT, WHEN HE WRITETH UP THE PEOPLE, THAT THIS MAN WAS BORN THERE. Selah. As well the singers as the players on instruments shall be there: ALL MY SPRINGS ARE IN THEE.

This Psalm reveals the awesome power for the salvation of souls within the Tabernacle Prayer. Verse 6 says that the Lord Himself shall count as He writes up the people! This shows that God records how many were born into the Kingdom of God by our king-priest ministry! Psalms 87 also tells of the love God has for this type of prayer, and the power and glorious benefits that go with it. It begins by saying, *"His foundation is in the holy mountains"*, and this means that there is strength and power in Zion. As we learned earlier, Mount Zion is the heavenly Jerusalem that we reach by praying according to Pattern. It is in this realm, the High Place of the Lord, where we have power to destroy our enemies. Verse 2 says, *"The LORD loveth the gates of Zion more than all the dwellings of Jacob"*. The *"dwellings of Jacob"* represent the Tabernacle of

Moses, but Zion represents the fulfillment and perfection of worship into the presence of God. Zion is the matrix or birthing place for the desires of God's heart for all of mankind. That's why verse 3 adds, *"Glorious things are spoken of thee, O city of God!"*

To further prove this point verse 4 says, *"I will make mention of Rahab and Babylon"*. The words *"Rahab"* and *"Babylon"* mean the proud and the confused. Then it says, *"behold Philistia and Tyre"*. The word *"behold"* means to watch and to take notice. *"Philistia"* means to roll, and to wallow self. That is one of our covenant promises, that God will roll or entwine Himself with us to give us the power of the Almighty! *"Tyre"* means a rock, which represents God the Almighty, and the One that came to build the family and House of God. Then it adds, *"with Ethiopia"*, which means Cush, or children of Ham. In summary this Psalm is saying that prayer according to Pattern will transform and save the proud, the confused, or in general the heathen nations!

According to verse 5, many will be born into the Kingdom of God from prayer that goes forth from Zion! No wonder God loves Zion! This beautiful Psalm ends with verse 7 saying, *"all my springs are in thee"*. The king-priests of the Lord who ascend into Mount Zion will have the living waters of God to bring in the end-time harvest!

Please don't let another day pass! All of His springs are in you, but they will not flow out and transform a lost and dying world unless you enter into your covenant as a king-priest. It is our desire to see true worshippers cover the earth. If you have been touched by this book and have decided to enter into your holy calling, we would like to know. Please visit our web site and register.   We have a global map that we use to mark places where people are praying according to Pattern.   We will one day fulfill our destiny to worship God in unity as one man!   The Body of Christ praying and worshipping according to Pattern can achieve this.   Let's pray the eternal purposes of God according to Ephesians 4:13, *"Till we all come in the unity of the faith, and of the knowledge of the Son of God, unto a perfect man, unto the measure of the stature of the fulness of Christ"*.

Numbers 6:24-26

The LORD bless thee, and keep thee: The LORD make his face shine upon thee, and be gracious unto thee: The LORD lift up his countenance upon thee, and give thee peace

From The Heart Of Sandy & C.J.

For a summarized version of how to
pray according to Pattern see the
companion booklet entitled:
**"The Power Of Prayer
According To The Pattern"**

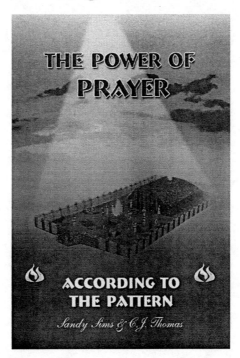

Visit our web site: www.myholycall.com
Email: prayer@myholycall.com